Social and Emotional Learning Activities

GRADES
5–6

Writing: Guadalupe Lopez
Kathleen Jorgensen
Bryan Langdo
Content Editing: Lisa Vitarisi Mathews
Teera Robinson
Copy Editing: Laurie Westrich
Art Direction: Yuki Meyer
Cover Design: Yuki Meyer
Illustration: Bryan Langdo
Design/Production: Jessica Onken

EMC 6098

Visit *teaching-standards.com* to view a correlation of this book.

Correlated to Current Standards

Congratulations on your purchase of some of the finest teaching materials in the world.

For information about other Evan-Moor products, call 1-800-777-4362, fax 1-800-777-4332, or visit our website, www.evan-moor.com.

10 Harris Court, Suite C-3, Monterey, CA 93940-5773. Printed in USA.

004

CPSIA: Sheridan Saline, Inc., Saline, MI, USA [4/2025]

CONTENTS

Introduction

Activities

What's in *Social and Emotional Learning Activities*?

9 Units of Engaging SEL Activities

Each unit has a different SEL focus and begins with a teacher page. The teacher page has an introduction to read aloud to students, should you choose to do so, and a list of the SEL skills covered in the unit.

The rest of the pages in the unit are reproducible activity pages for students. Some activity pages have a focus box at the top. It provides context to help students understand the SEL skill practiced on that page.

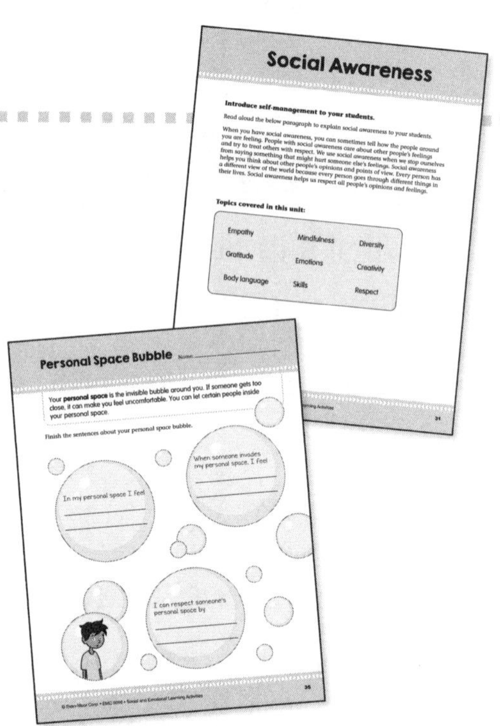
Social Awareness

Introduce self-management to your students.

Read aloud the below paragraph to explain social awareness to your students.

When you have social awareness, you can sometimes tell how the people around you are feeling. People with social awareness care about other people's feelings and try to treat others with respect. We use social awareness when we stop ourselves from saying something that might hurt someone else's feelings. Social awareness helps you think about other people's opinions and points of view. Every person has a different view of the world because every person goes through different things in their lives. Social awareness helps us respect all people's opinions and feelings.

Topics covered in this unit:

Empathy, Mindfulness, Diversity, Gratitude, Emotions, Creativity, Body language, Skills, Respect

31

Personal Space Bubble Name: ____

Your **personal space** is the invisible bubble around you. If someone gets too close, it can make you feel uncomfortable. You can let certain people inside your personal space.

Finish the sentences about your personal space bubble.

In my personal space I feel ____

When someone invades my personal space, I feel ____

I can respect someone's personal space by ____

35

The Activities

The activities are designed to be engaging and open-ended, with a wide variety of response formats. The goal is for students to feel like the activity is providing a "safe space" to let their own unique viewpoint and creativity shine through. For most activities there are no incorrect answers because each student will have a different world view and a different experience. Activity formats include the following:

- hypothetical scenarios and problem solving
- making choices and justifying opinions
- creative writing and drawing
- mazes, puzzles, and games
- critical thinking
- visual information
- art projects
- interactive games

Answer Key

For most of the activities in this book, answers will vary. For some activities, a sample answer or correct answer is provided in the answer key section of the book.

How to Use This Book

Planning Instruction

The units in this book and the pages within each unit do not have to be taught in sequential order. Choose the units and/or pages that align with your students' needs.

Note that each unit begins with a teacher's page that has an optional introduction to read aloud to students.

How to Use *Social and Emotional Learning Activities*

Reproduce Each Activity and Distribute It to Students
Have students complete an activity to supplement learning during the school day. Or assign an activity to students as homework.

Use Activities to Guide Whole-Group Discussion
There are different ways to use an activity for a whole-group discussion. You can review student answers as a group after each student completes the activity individually. Or you can use the information in the focus box or the items on the page as a conversation starter.

Use Activities for Small-Group Discussions
Have students talk about their answers and reflect on the activity with a partner or with a small group.

About Social and Emotional Learning

Social and emotional learning (SEL) focuses on the skills we use every day to maintain healthy relationships, manage our behavior, form goals, communicate with others, persevere through challenging situations, reflect on our emotions, and make decisions. One goal of SEL is to empower learners by helping them develop confidence in their own judgment. Research shows that SEL can promote academic and career success. It can also help learners deal with daily stressors.

What Are SEL Skills?

These are some of the skills that are gained and reinforced by SEL:

- empathizing
- making responsible choices
- developing grit
- accepting personal responsibility
- conflict resolution
- setting and achieving goals
- maintaining focus
- mindfulness
- constructive communication
- evaluating possible outcomes
- monitoring self-talk
- developing healthy coping methods
- demonstrating flexibility
- optimistic thinking
- cooperation
- monitoring expectations

Evan-Moor's Approach to SEL

The activities in this book are designed to be culturally responsive and considerate of the cultural diversity found in the classroom and in the world around us. The messaging in this book seeks to avoid labeling any feelings as *wrong* or *bad*. Instead, we appeal to students' abilities to think creatively, critically, reflectively, and empathically. We believe that SEL skills can be practiced and applied in daily life.

Self-Awareness

Introduce self-awareness to your students.

Self-awareness is knowing your own feelings and thoughts and knowing yourself. You can think about how your feelings affect what you do and say. You can practice self-awareness by thinking about things you are good at and things you would like to do better. Another part of self-awareness is knowing what you value, or what is important to you. When you have self-awareness, you take time to think about how you view yourself and how you want other people to view you. Another part of self-awareness is figuring out how certain things make you feel. Self-awareness is really about trying to know and understand yourself.

Topics covered in this unit:

Character	Mindfulness	Curiosity
Gratitude	Emotions	Creativity
Responsibility	Skills	Self-talk

My Character Infographic

Name: ____________________

Character is the collection of traits that describe you. What words do people think of when they think of you? What words do you think of when you think of yourself?

Infographics use pictures, charts, and text to provide information about a topic. The infographic below gives information about Reeva's character.

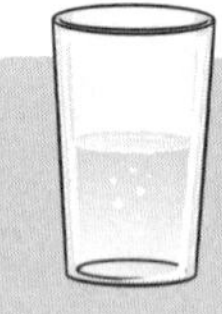

If you ask me, the glass is always half full.

I'm curious by nature—I love to learn new things.

I have good friends, but I'm usually quiet around new people.

I don't like to quit. When things get hard, I work hard!

Think about your own character. What do you have in common with Reeva? How are you different from her?

My Character Infographic, continued

Name: ______________________

Make an infographic that tells about your character. Draw pictures and write statements that are true about yourself. Be creative!

All About Me

Name: ____________________

Complete the chart about yourself.

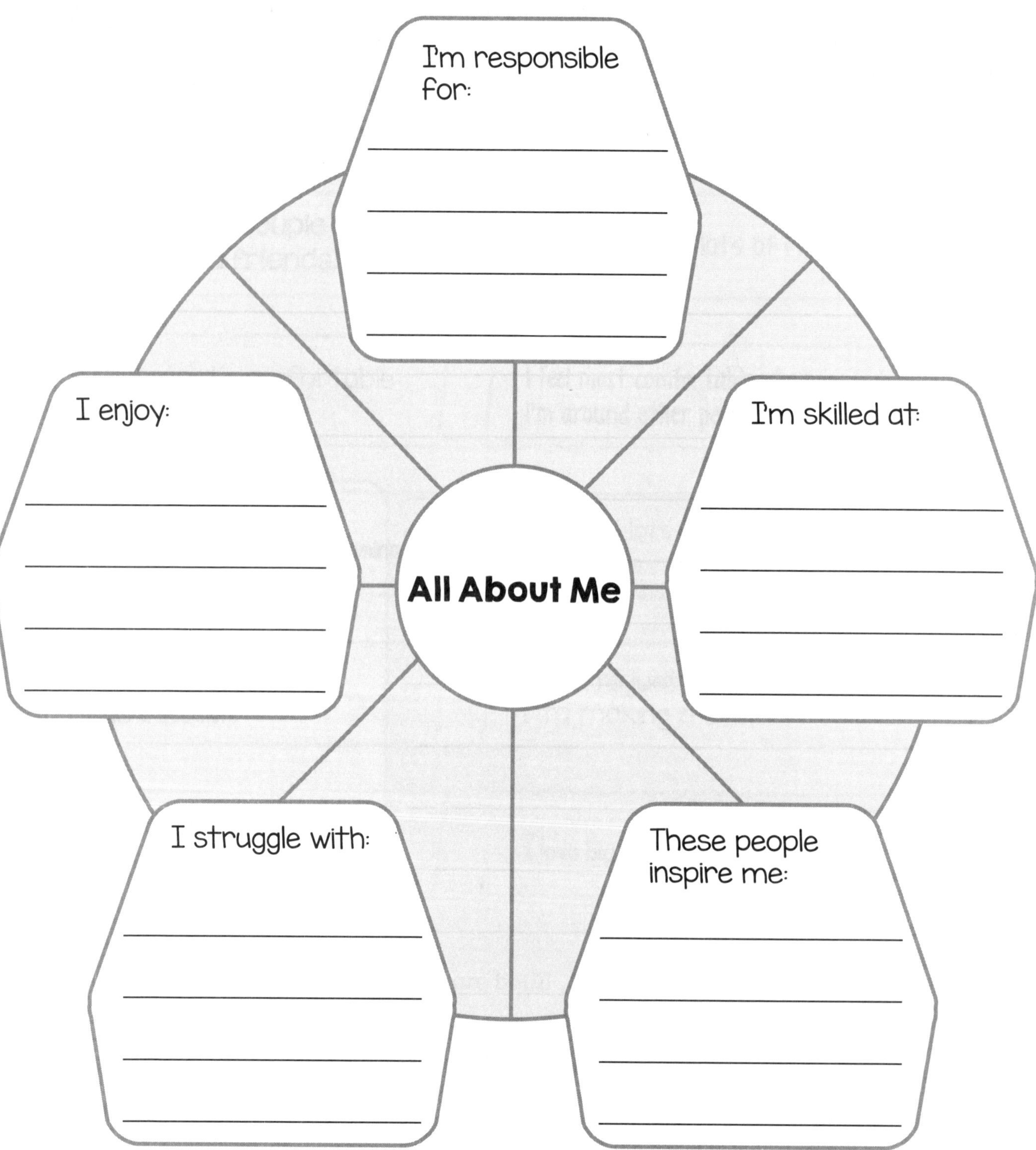

Positive Emotions

Name: ______________________________

Experiencing positive emotions is good for our physical and mental health. We can seek out positive emotions just as we seek out nutritious food to put into our bodies.

These six words describe positive emotions. For each word, write about an activity that helps you experience that emotion.

Joyful

Grateful

Peaceful

Creative

Confident

Playful

My Social Traits

Name: ______________________________

There are some social traits you try to do, and some you try not to do. It is important to recognize your own social traits. Read the lists of social traits below. Write a check mark next to the ones that you do sometimes.

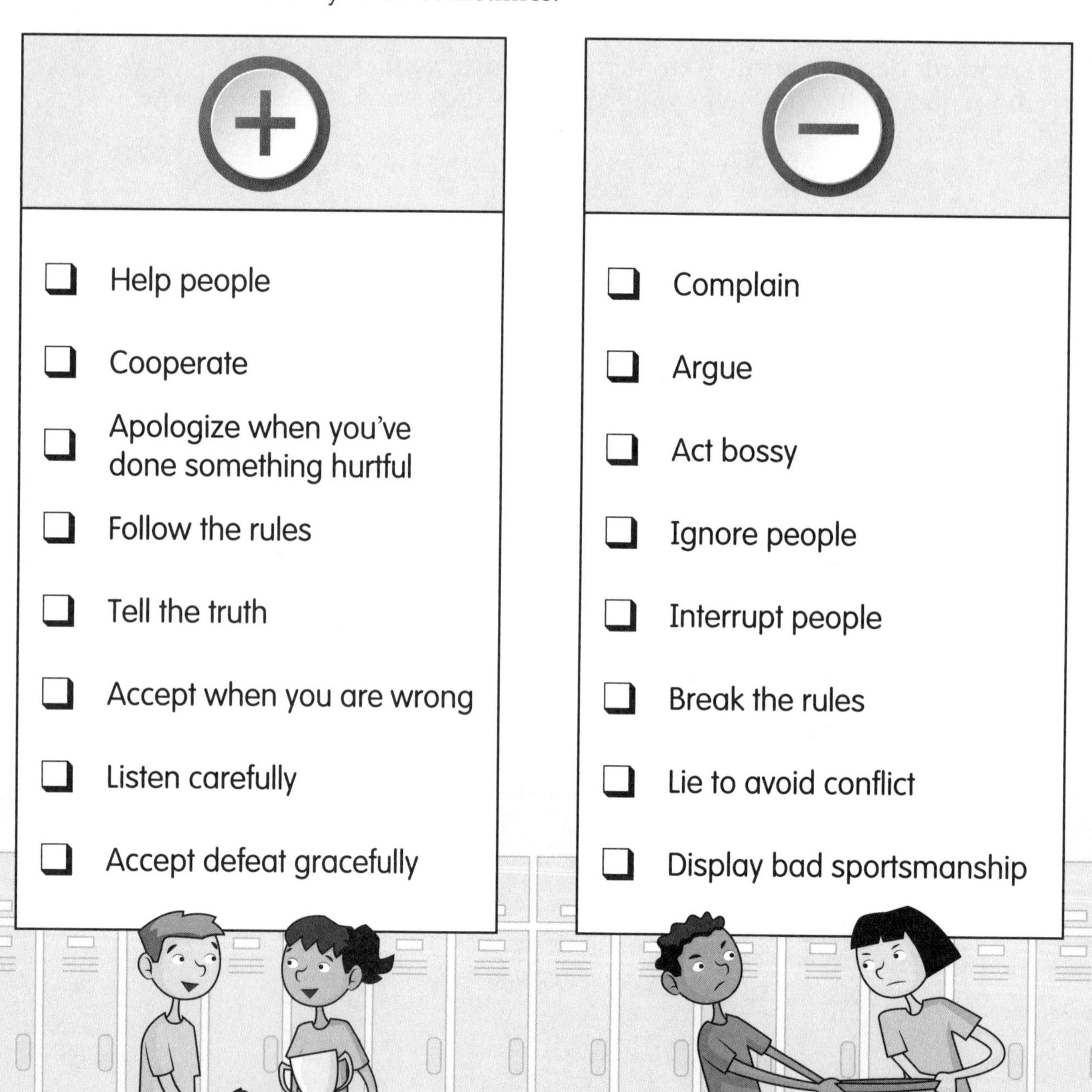

+

- ❑ Help people
- ❑ Cooperate
- ❑ Apologize when you've done something hurtful
- ❑ Follow the rules
- ❑ Tell the truth
- ❑ Accept when you are wrong
- ❑ Listen carefully
- ❑ Accept defeat gracefully

−

- ❑ Complain
- ❑ Argue
- ❑ Act bossy
- ❑ Ignore people
- ❑ Interrupt people
- ❑ Break the rules
- ❑ Lie to avoid conflict
- ❑ Display bad sportsmanship

My Traits

Name: ____________________

Circle four traits that describe you. Then write one in each gray box. Inside the white boxes, write about a time when you showed each trait.

calm	funny	friendly	responsible
serious	cheerful	creative	hardworking

Thoughts About Myself

Name: ____________________

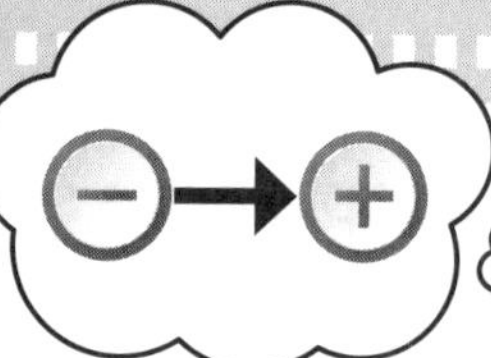

All people have thoughts about themselves. It is important to try to pay attention to the thoughts you have about yourself and recognize what you like about yourself.

In the shape, write a **negative thought** that you sometimes have about yourself. Then write a **positive thought** to replace it.

Negative Thought **Positive Thought**

1.

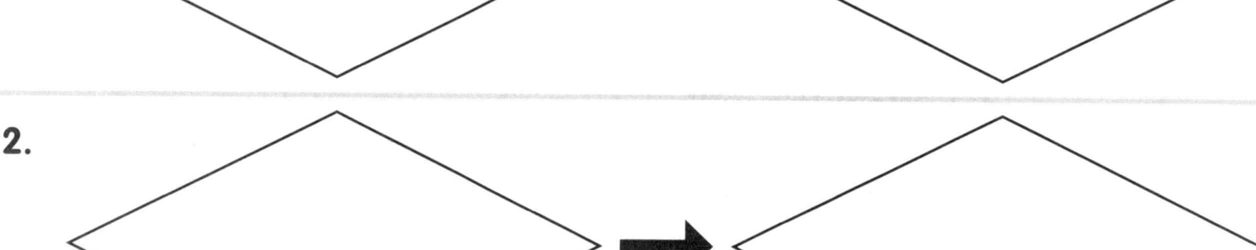

2.

3.

4.

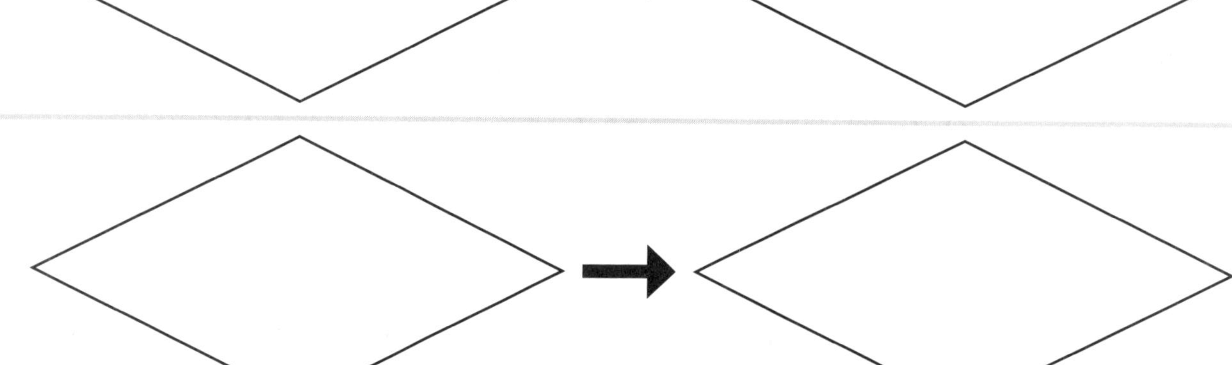

Self-Management

Introduce self-management to your students.

Read aloud the below paragraph to explain self-management to your students.

Self-management is about making choices that you feel are helpful to you and to others. When you practice self-management, you think about how you want to treat others and yourself. You think about your behavior. And you think about things you want to do better. For example, some people want to be kinder to others. Some people want to get better grades in school. And some people want to be a good friend. Think about what kind of person you want to be. Think about what you want to do better. Then think about what choices you can make to do that. You have the power to make good choices. As long as you are trying to be kind and respectful when you make a choice, you are doing great.

Topics covered in this unit:

Self-control	Mindfulness	Goals
Gratitude	Emotions	Creativity
Respect	Self-care	Self-talk

Your Self-Talk

Name: ______________________________

When you talk to yourself in your head, those thoughts are called **self-talk**. Negative self-talk is when you say things to yourself to make yourself feel not so great or to discourage yourself. Positive self-talk gives you confidence.

Each person below is worried about something. Look at the person and read the thought bubble. In the speech bubble, write positive self-talk for the person.

Draw a picture or paste a photograph of yourself in the box. In the thought bubble, write a worrying thought you sometimes have. Then write positive self-talk for yourself in the speech bubble.

Reaching a Goal

Name: ________________________

It's great to have goals. Winning a race, doing well on a test, and being able to play the piano are goals. But just setting a goal isn't enough. You also need a plan. A plan helps you practice and do what you need to do so that you will be able to reach your goal.

Read the story.

Ryu was very quiet. He wanted to be more comfortable speaking up in class and answering the teacher's questions. To reach that goal, he made a plan. For the first week, he would raise his hand to answer a question just one time, even if he felt nervous. During the second week, he would raise his hand on two days. During the third week, he would raise his hand three days, and so on.

What was Ryu's goal?

What actions did Ryu take to accomplish his goal?

Shawnda wants to learn how to play the trumpet.
Make a plan with three actions that she can do to accomplish this goal.

#1	#2	#3

Calm-Down Strategies

Name: ______________________________

We can try to use our senses to feel calm when we feel anxious or upset. Read the calm-down strategies in the circles below. On the line inside each circle, write one more example of something that might make you feel calm.

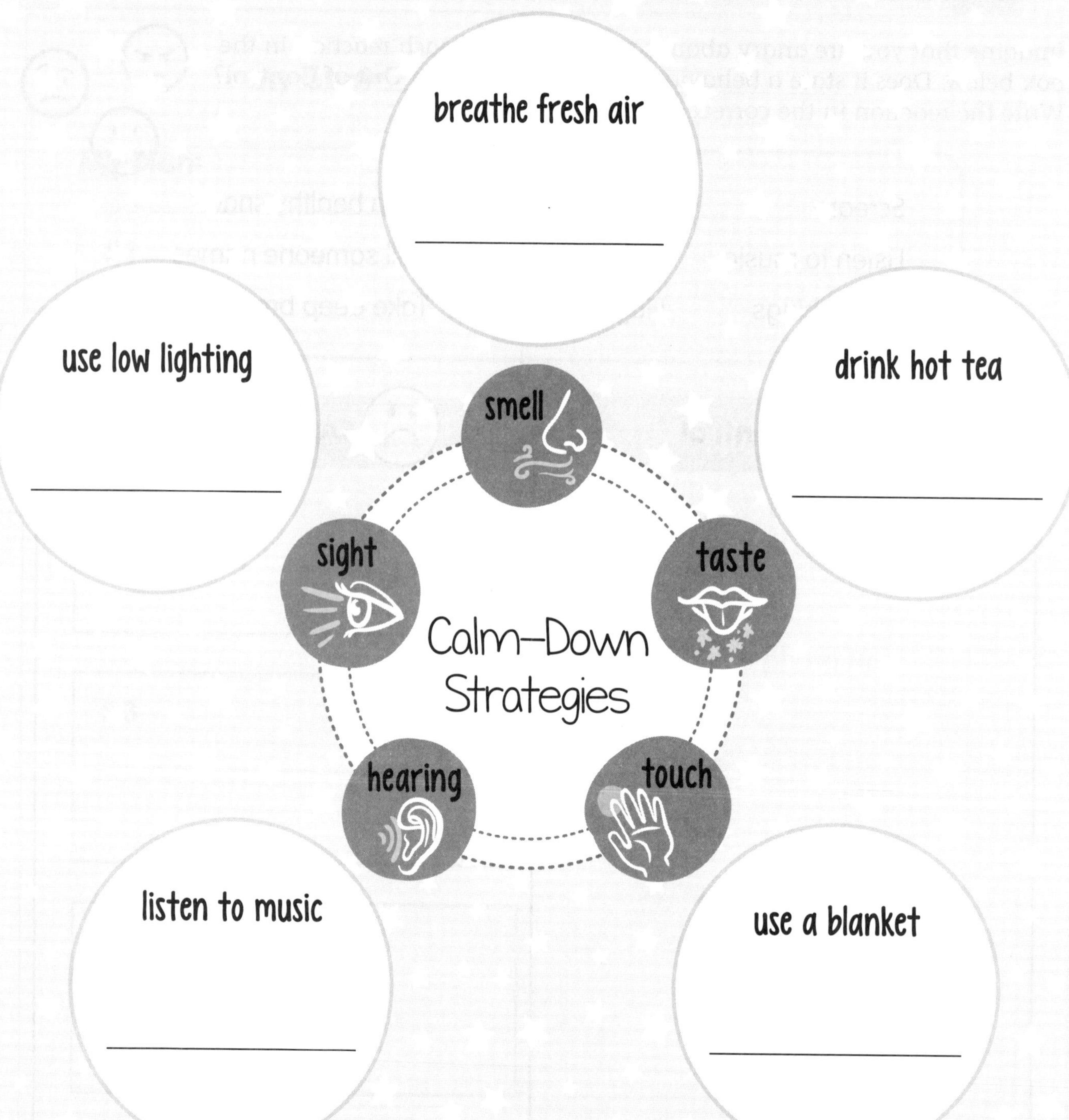

Respectfully Disagree

Name: ______________________

Sometimes we disagree with someone. When we have a difficult conversation with another person, we can still try to be respectful.

Rewrite each statement to be more respectful.

You always ignore me!	→	
You never text me back!	→	
Stop being a cry baby!	→	
This is your fault!	→	

Self-Care, continued

Name: ______________________

On page 27, some of the letters in the list are bold. When the bold letters are put together, they will form the words in the sentence below. Write the bold letters in order from left to right on the lines below.

___ ___ ___ ___ ___   ___ ___ ___

___ ___ ___ ___ ___ ___   ___ ___ ___   ___ ___

___ ___ ___   ___ ___ ___ ___-___ ___ ___ ___.

Now follow the instruction that you wrote above. Write two things you do for self-care. Then draw a picture of yourself doing self-care in the box.

1. ______________________________

2. ______________________________

Be Mindful

Name: ____________________

When we are **mindful**, or we practice **mindfulness**, we are trying to pay attention to our thoughts and feelings. We try to observe how our body feels. We try to understand the emotions we are experiencing. Sometimes people blame themselves for having certain feelings. But when you are mindful, you do not blame yourself for having any feelings. You simply try to understand what you are feeling so that you can know if you are okay.

Read about what the person is going through. Then write about a time that you went through something similar or felt something similar.

When Megan was with her whole family, one of her cousins made a joke about her clothes. Megan felt embarrassed. She felt her face get red hot. She wished she could hide.

____

____

____

The words in each box tell what someone is going through. Color the box if it tells about something you can relate to or if it reminds you of something that has happened to you before.

The gym teacher is making everyone dance. Alejandro is terrified. He doesn't like how he dances.

Terry is nervous to do his speech. His hands feel sweaty.

Fan Liu can't focus during class. She feels so sleepy. She keeps feeling her eyes close.

Even though it's the middle of the night, Lamar can't sleep. He can't stop thinking about what he has to do tomorrow. His heart is beating fast.

Empathy

Name: ___________________________

When you have **empathy**, you try to understand how someone else feels. You do not have to know someone to **empathize** with them. Anyone can try to have empathy for another person. You can even have empathy for someone you disagree with.

Read about what each person is going through. Then write two emotions that you think this person might be feeling.

Tony kept chatting during class. He wasn't paying attention. Then the teacher called on him to answer a question. Tony said he didn't know the answer. "Pay attention," the teacher said sternly in front of everybody.

____

____

Asta's grandpa asked **Asta** to come over after school and help him in the garden. Asta told him she was busy, but she wasn't being honest. That day, he came over to Asta's house and saw her watching TV after school. Asta didn't know what to say to her grandpa.

____

____

Dominic and his friend got into an argument. Dominic feels like the argument was his friend's fault.

____

____

Twylah saw a girl named May getting bullied at school. Twylah didn't do anything to stop the bullying. She had never talked to May before. But Twylah didn't think anybody deserved to be bullied, ever.

____

____

Social Awareness

Introduce social awareness to your students.

Read aloud the below paragraph to explain social awareness to your students.

When you have social awareness, you can sometimes tell how the people around you are feeling. People with social awareness care about other people's feelings and try to treat others with respect. We use social awareness when we stop ourselves from saying something that might hurt someone else's feelings. Social awareness helps you think about other people's opinions and points of view. Every person has a different view of the world because every person goes through different things in their life. Social awareness helps us respect all people's opinions and feelings.

Topics covered in this unit:

Empathy	Mindfulness	Diversity
Gratitude	Emotions	Creativity
Body language	Skills	Respect

Lucy and Eva

Name: ______________________

Read the story. Then answer the items.

Lucy was watching her four-year-old sister, Eva, while their dad took a shower. Eva never sat still. Eva was hungry and wanted a cheese sandwich. While Lucy made the sandwich, Eva twirled around the kitchen. Lucy cut the sandwich into squares and placed it on the table.

"Nope," said Eva, shaking her head. "Mommy always cuts it into triangles."

"Eva, no matter how we cut it, it's still a cheese sandwich," sighed Lucy. "Eat it."

Lucy sat across from Eva and rested her chin on her hand. She made sure Eva ate the sandwich. Lucy looked at the clock on the wall. Dad had been in the shower for 10 minutes. "When will he be done?" she thought.

1. Write three feelings that you think Lucy is feeling while watching Eva.

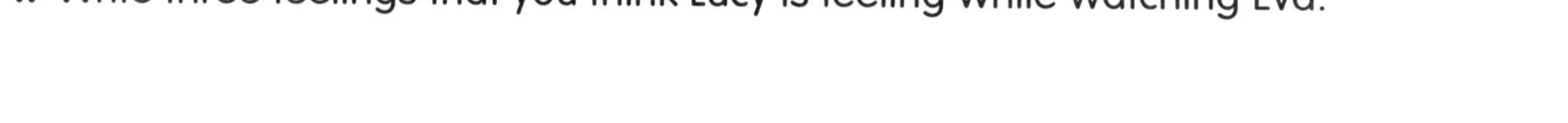

2. Draw a picture to show a time when you felt the same way Lucy did in this story.

Personal Space Bubble

Name: ______________________

Your **personal space** is the invisible bubble around you. If someone gets too close, it can make you feel uncomfortable. However, you can let certain people inside your personal space.

Finish the sentences about your personal space bubble.

When someone invades my personal space, I feel

____

____

____

In my personal space, I feel

____

____

____

I can respect someone's personal space by

____

____

____

Social Cues

Name: ____________________

Finish each sentence. Write the word in the crossword.

Down

1. When people are annoyed, they roll their _____.
2. When you _____ your head, it means "no."
3. Social cues include body _____.
4. A finger to the lips says, "Be _____."

Across

5. A smile may signal _____.
6. A synonym of "embrace" is _____.
7. Raised eyebrows signal _____.
8. Crossed arms together with a frown could possibly signal _____.

Appreciating Diversity

Name: ______________________

People come from different backgrounds and cultures. This is what creates diversity.

Use the Venn diagram to compare yourself to one person you know. You can include information about race, religion, personality traits, interests, or culture. In the overlapping section, include details that you have in common. List as many details as you can.

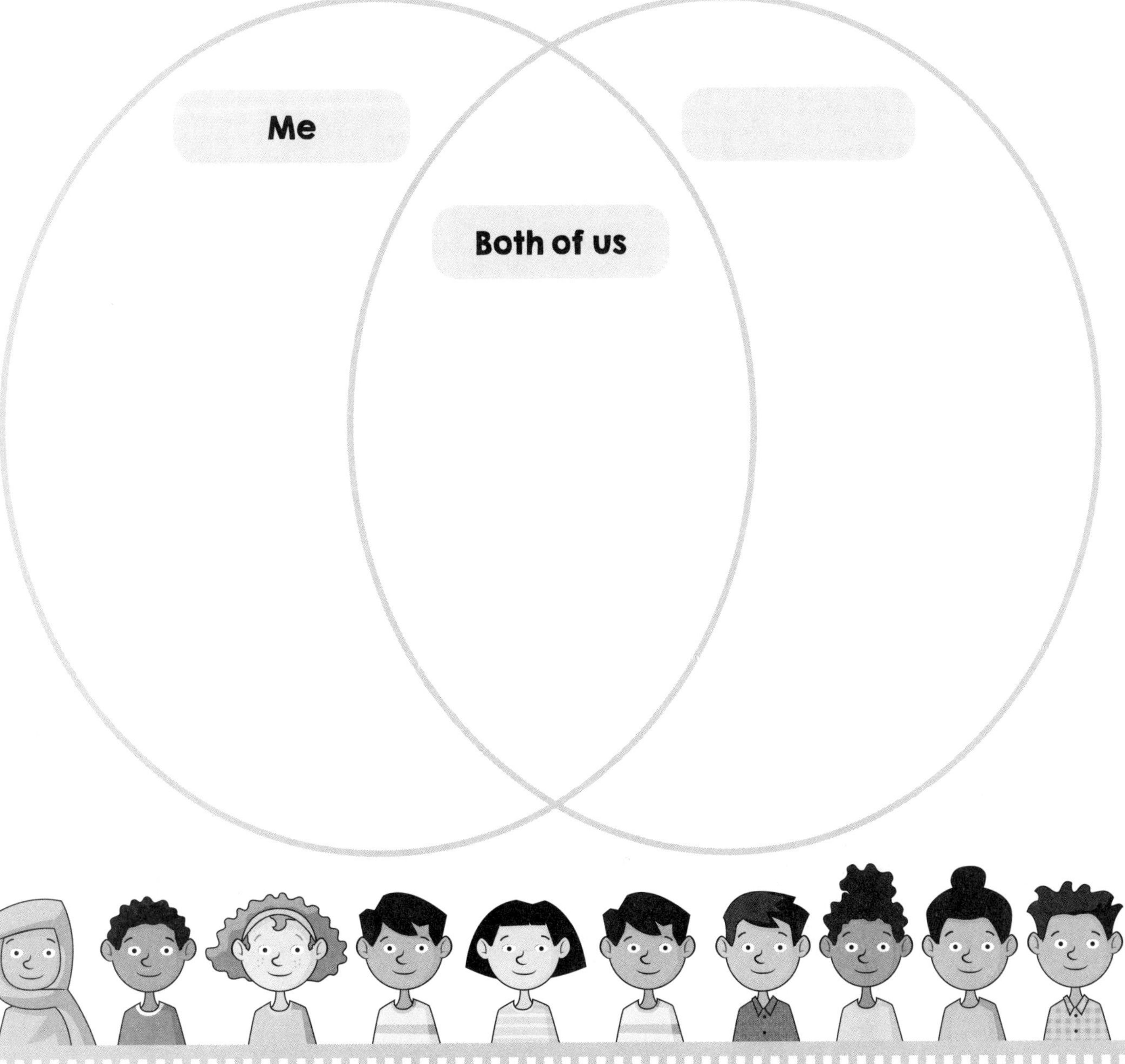

Appreciating Diversity, continued

Name: ______________________

An acrostic poem has one word that goes from top to bottom. Each of its letters forms part of a word or phrase. Here's an example:

Cute and clever
Animals
That like to
Sleep all day

Choose one of the words from the word bank. Or you can use a word you think of. Then write an acrostic poem that celebrates diversity. Write the letters of the word you choose in the boxes. Then write the poem.

DIVERSE	LOVE	COLORS	RAINBOW	PEOPLE
WELCOME	ACCEPT	HUMAN	TOGETHER	UNITED

☐ ______________________
☐ ______________________
☐ ______________________
☐ ______________________
☐ ______________________
☐ ______________________
☐ ______________________
☐ ______________________

Donate to Help Others

Name: ____________________

A philanthropist is someone who tries to help improve the well-being of other people. Many philanthropists are wealthy, and they donate money to help people and organizations. But you don't need money to be a philanthropist. You can donate items, or you can donate your time and skills.

Look around your home for items you could donate. Think about your schedule and when you have free time. Think about things you're good at or things you could do to help other people. Read the examples in the chart. Then write your own answers in the chart.

Things I can donate	My free time	My skills
Example: clothes	Example: every afternoon	Example: Reading. I could read to younger kids.

I Can Help

Name: ______________________

Think of three problems in your town, in your school, or even just among your friends. They can be big problems or small problems.

For each problem, write one idea for how you could help solve the problem.

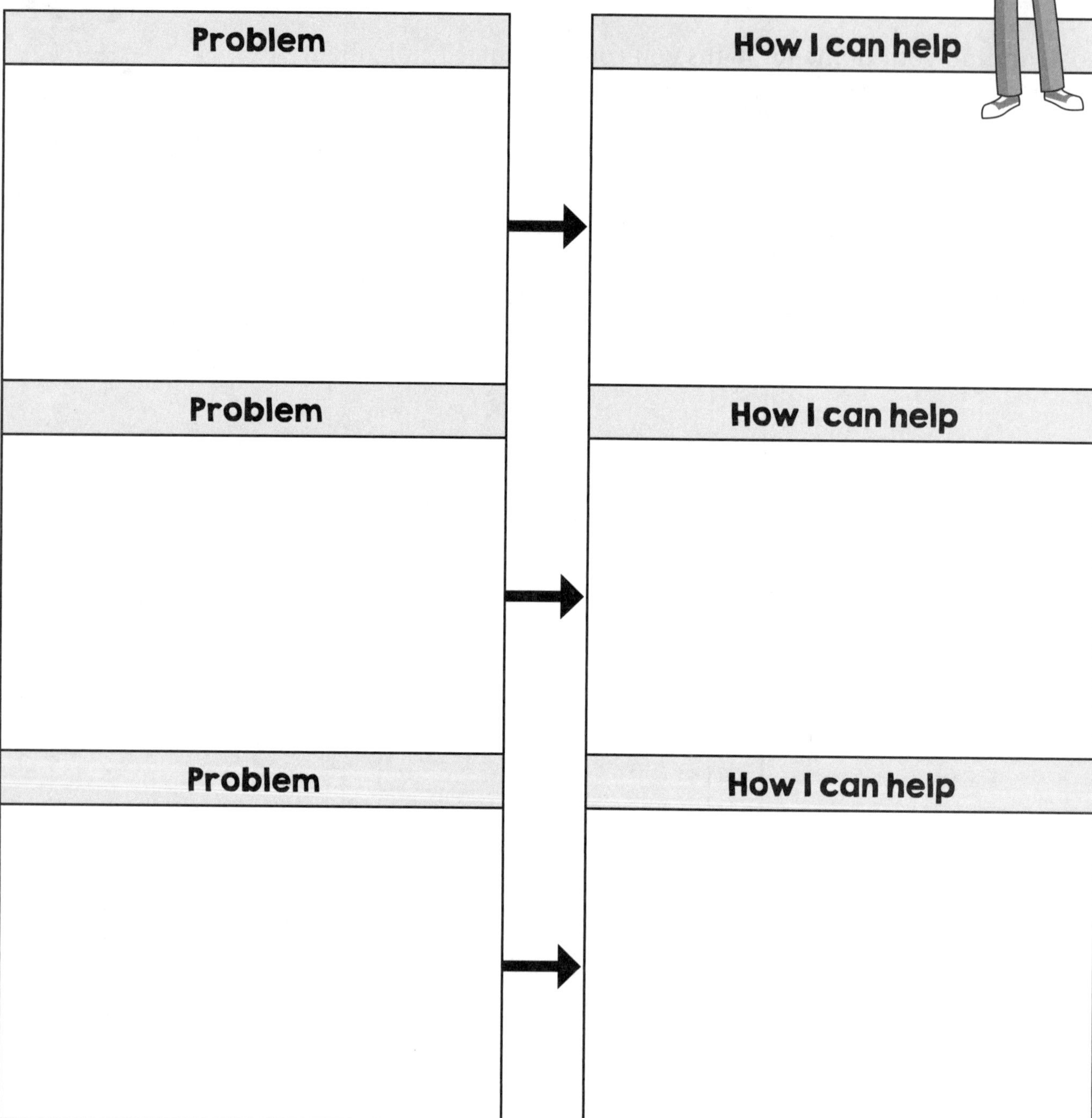

Okay and Not Okay

Name: ______________________

We all have opinions. It is okay to state your opinions, even if you disagree with others. But it is not okay to be disrespectful or to say things that are unkind and **uninformed**, or not based on facts.

Read the comment. Then color the circle to tell whether the comment is **okay** or **not okay** to say.

1. All people from that ethnic group have big noses.

○ okay ○ not okay

2. Well, everyone has their own unique style of speaking.

○ okay ○ not okay

3. You know, she is probably very lazy. All people who look like she does are lazy.

○ okay ○ not okay

4. 

Every person's body is different. The world is made up of different body types!

○ okay ○ not okay

How to Handle It

Name: ______________________________

When we are **productive**, we are trying to make progress and get stuff done. We can choose to communicate with others in a productive way, or in a way that helps solve a problem or helps us to understand each other.

Read about the situation. Then write inside the boxes to tell what happened that was **productive** and what was **not productive**.

1. Wendy stormed into her brother's bedroom and called him a mean name. He was surprised. She kept yelling at him. His feelings were hurt, but in a calm voice he gently said to Wendy, "I want to talk about this, but we should wait until we can have a calm conversation."

PRODUCTIVE

2. At dinner, Nacho's parents said they had a serious question to ask him. "Nacho, we are not accusing you of anything," said Nacho's dad. "Mr. Fox said you were throwing rocks at his mailbox. Is this true?" Nacho didn't say anything. "You can be honest with us, Honey," said his mom. Nacho got up from his chair and stomped out of the room without saying a word.

PRODUCTIVE

NOT PRODUCTIVE

Responsible Decision-Making

Introduce responsible decision-making to your students.

Read aloud the below paragraph to explain responsible decision-making to your students.

You have the power to make choices and decisions. When you do responsible decision-making, you try to make choices that are constructive, or helpful. You think about the results of your choices. You think about other people's feelings and how your choices will affect other people. You also think about how your choices will affect you later on. Think about the choices you make every day. You probably make some choices for your health. You probably make some choices for your safety. And you probably make a lot of choices because of how you feel. It is okay to use your feelings to help guide your choices. Try to also think about the feelings of others and what could happen after you make a choice.

Topics covered in this unit:

Character	Mindfulness	Curiosity
Gratitude	Emotions	Creativity
Responsibility	Skills	Self-talk

So Awkward

Name: ______________________

When a situation is **awkward**, or weird, it can be hard to know what to do. Even in an awkward situation, it is important to treat everyone with respect.

Read about the situation that happened with Brady and Faizan. Then answer the items.

Brady asked Faizan if he wanted to go to the school volleyball game together on Friday. Brady said his parents could drive. Faizan said he wasn't going to go because his sister was coming home from college this weekend, and he wanted to spend time with her. On Friday afternoon, though, Faizan's sister said she couldn't come home to visit. So Faizan asked his dad to drive him to the volleyball game. Once he got to the school, his friend Janessa saw him and called him over to sit with her friends. Faizan was having fun sitting with Janessa and her friends, when suddenly he felt a tap on his shoulder. "Thought you weren't coming to the game!" Faizan turned to see Brady sitting right behind him on the bleachers. He looked kind of angry, but also like his feelings were hurt. Faizan just said "I, uh." He didn't know what to say.

1. Write one thing that Faizan could say to make the situation better, or less awkward.

____

____

2. Write one thing that Faizan could say to make the situation worse, or more awkward.

____

____

Weird Situations

Name: ______________________

Everybody gets into weird situations sometimes. You may feel weird because of something someone else says or does. And sometimes you may feel like you said or did something that other people will think is weird.

Look at the pictures that show weird situations. Write an **X** in the circle under the picture if a situation like this has ever happened to you.

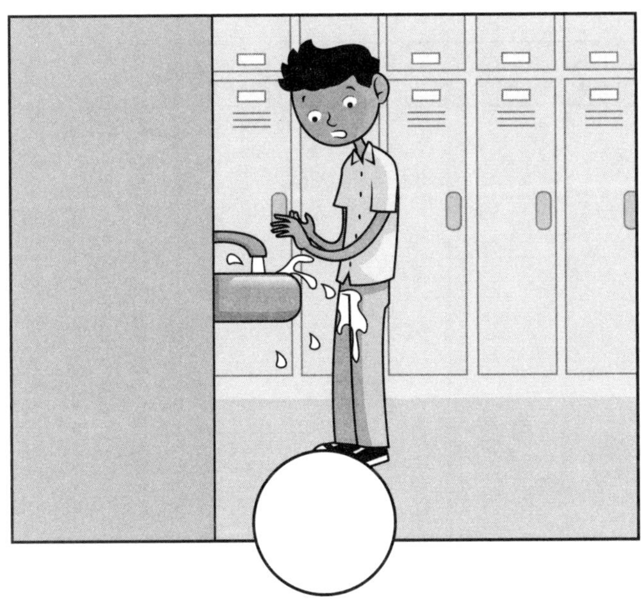

Printer Problem

Name: ______________________

Imagine that you are printing a page at your school library. Your print job has finished printing. As you collect your page, you notice that the machine says the paper has run out. This means that the next person's print job will not print.

Describe three ways you could choose to respond to this situation. Then write a possible **consequence**, or result, of each choice.

Decision 1	Decision 2	Decision 3

Consequence 1	Consequence 2	Consequence 3

Decisions, Decisions

Name: ______________________________

Imagine that your class took a test. Most students got 7 out of 10 as a score. The teacher said that students can retake the test, but if they do, they have to keep the grade they earn, even if it is worse than the first grade they earned. What would you do?

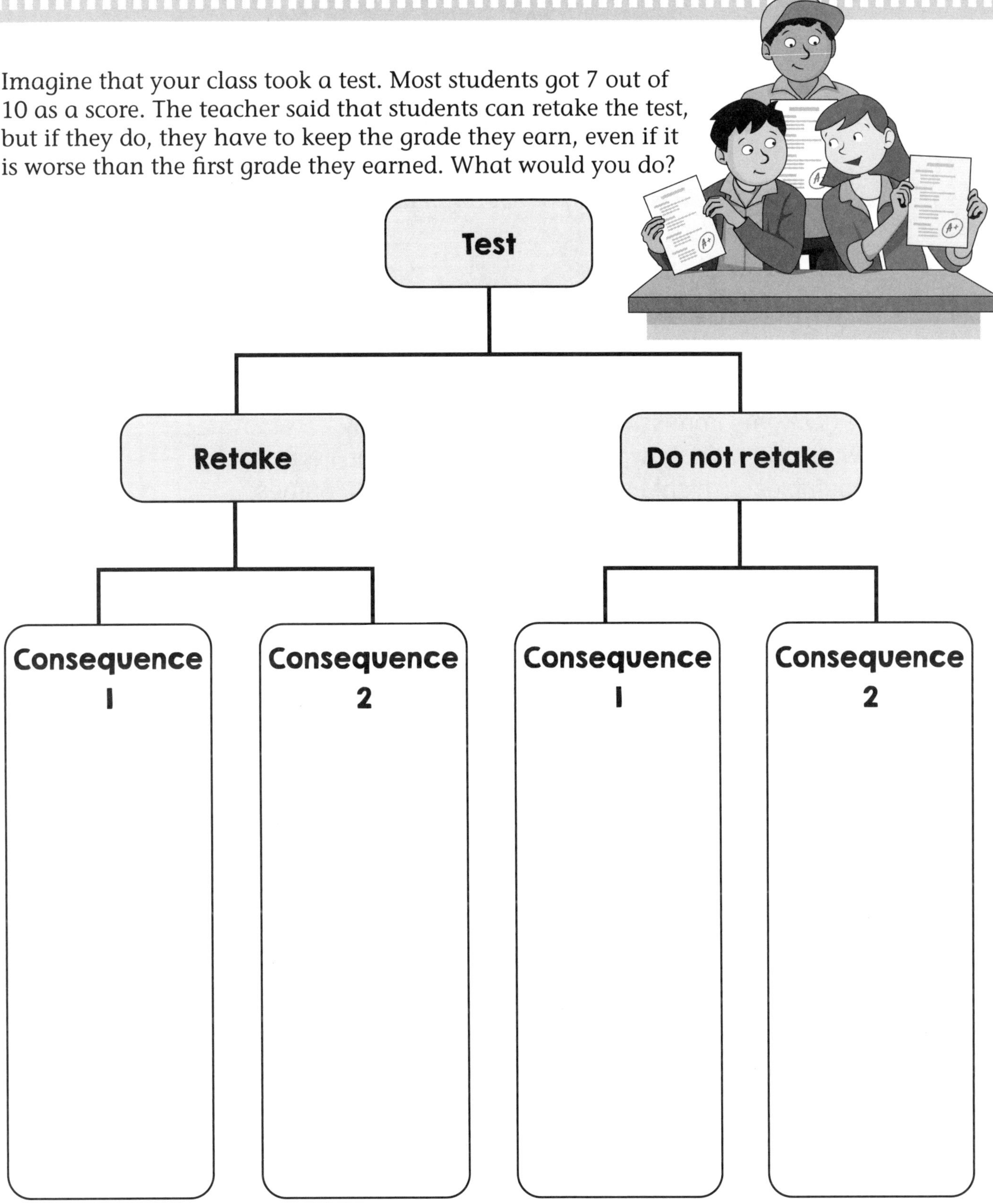

Habits I Choose

Name: ___________________________

A **habit** is something you do often, and sometimes you do it without even thinking about it. Some habits are healthier than others. We can choose our habits.

Read what each person says about his or her own habits. Then rate each on a scale from 1 to 5 stars.

1 = not healthy   5 = very healthy

1. Juliette:
When I get home from school, I stay inside. I do my homework and look at my phone until dinner. I don't eat any vegetables. At night I stay up late playing video games.

2. Amir:
I wake up and eat breakfast. After school, I play in the yard with my dog. After I finish doing my homework, I watch TV for a little while. Then I brush my teeth and read before bed.

3. Mei:
I skip breakfast because I always wake up late and I don't want to miss my bus. At lunch I eat snacks, usually chips or small cakes that come in a package. I refuse to eat any kid of sandwich, fruit, or vegetable. After school, I do chores. I like to keep my bedroom tidy.

Habits I Choose, continued

Name: ___________________________

Write two habits you have that make you feel good or healthy.

1.

2.

Write two habits you have that you think you could change so that you could feel better or more healthy.

1.

2.

Draw a picture of one thing you do every day or every week that you are proud of.

Many Ways to Cope

Name: ______________________

Coping is what people do when they go through a difficult time. There are many things people can choose to do to help them cope.

Read about what Samar is going through in each circle. Then color the square that tells the way you would choose to cope if you were Samar.

1. Samar is working on a school project with a partner, Tara. But Tara is not listening to any of his ideas.

- Samar can try writing about his feelings in a journal.
- Samar can try screaming at Tara.

2. Samar is riding bikes with Jordan and Parminder. Jordan is in a bad mood, and he keeps snapping at Samar, which is making Samar mad.

- Samar can stop playing with his friends and go home.
- Samar can try telling Jordan how he feels.

Each cloud states a different way that people cope. Read them, and color the ones that state a way that you have coped when you were going through a difficult time or felt upset.

3.

- **slam doors**
- **yell**
- **write**
- **read**
- **make something**
- **exercise**

Making Tough Choices

Name: ____________________

Think about a time when you had to make a tough decision. What was the problem? How did you feel? How did you decide what to do? Now pretend someone made a movie about it. In the box below, draw an exciting poster for this movie. Create a title for the movie.

Movie Title: ____________________

Helping Others

Name: ____________________

What do you do when other people are going through a tough time? Finish the chart. First read about the situation. Then write what you would do to help.

Situation	One thing you could do to try to help
1. Your family member is crying when you come home from school.	
2. Your friend is being rude to you. You know that your friend has been going through a tough time at home lately.	
3. You are at your grandparents' house. Your grandmother can't do some things that she used to be able to do. She asks for help with getting up, walking, and lifting items.	
4. Your neighbor knocked on the door. She is very worried because her dog ran out of the yard and is missing.	

My Responsibilities

Name: ______________________________

When you are responsible, you do what is expected of you or what you expect of yourself. We have responsibilities in all areas of our lives.

Write 2 responsibilities you have in each area of your life.

My Responsibilities

To myself

At home

In my community

At school

Dog Dilemma

Name: ____________________

Imagine that your friend invited you to her house for the first time. This is a new friend, and you want this to be a lasting friendship. There's just one problem. She has a dog, and you're afraid of dogs. What can you do?

Decision 1	Decision 2	Decision 3

Describe the consequence of each decision.

Consequence 1	Consequence 2	Consequence 3

Which was the best decision? Circle one: **1** **2** **3**

Why?

____

____

Relationship Skills

Introduce relationship skills to your students.

Relationship skills help us to have caring relationships with other people. We can practice habits that help us to communicate with others in a respectful way. We can also practice being understanding of others. Relationship skills help us tell other people that we disagree in a friendly way. They help us to be kind to the people we care about. The more we practice these skills, the better our relationships can be. These skills are all about having good conversations and relationships with others.

Topics covered in this unit:

Emotions	Inclusion	Mindfulness
Creativity	Body language	Empathy
Personal space	Communication	Acceptance
Manners	Cultural differences	Rules

Friendship Proverbs

Name: ______________________

A **proverb** is a wise saying that may give advice or tell an idea that many people believe is true.

The proverbs below are about friendship. Read each proverb. Then write what you think it means.

A friend in need is a friend indeed.

1. ______________________

____

You are known by the company you keep.

2. ______________________

____

Birds of a feather flock together.

3. ______________________

____

A friend to all is a friend to none.

4. ______________________

____

Qualities of a Good Friend

Name: ____________________________

The words in the box list the traits of a good friend.
Find the words in the puzzle and circle them.

intelligent	curious	trustworthy	protective	loyal	attentive
forgiving	energetic	humorous	generous	cheerful	honest
considerate	athletic	empathetic	quiet		

N	Y	J	F	K	X	I	M	G	X	P	M	F	Z	H	C	C	E	U	M
Y	Y	F	L	O	T	Q	T	T	S	Y	J	H	V	C	H	X	M	K	U
I	W	H	Y	L	W	R	E	A	L	J	W	U	Q	T	E	U	P	R	S
X	H	U	J	B	E	R	U	L	K	Z	Z	D	C	N	E	L	A	Q	U
V	Q	M	Y	O	Z	C	N	S	Y	V	O	B	Q	U	R	O	T	H	B
O	I	O	M	V	Y	U	K	S	T	D	U	U	I	N	F	L	H	E	Y
Y	N	R	R	U	E	Z	I	Y	Y	W	Q	C	Y	F	U	P	E	C	A
Q	T	O	K	D	I	U	J	Z	E	P	O	G	Y	B	L	L	T	U	T
U	E	U	E	C	K	G	R	T	Q	D	O	R	W	Z	B	Y	I	R	H
I	L	S	Q	N	F	F	P	G	C	F	Z	H	T	U	V	A	C	I	L
E	L	L	R	Q	E	L	C	R	E	U	O	A	O	H	M	B	J	O	E
T	I	O	O	D	A	R	B	W	O	N	S	R	B	N	Y	R	E	U	T
F	G	L	L	I	T	Y	G	P	W	T	E	J	G	G	E	L	J	S	I
K	E	J	O	Z	T	X	Z	E	C	R	E	R	E	I	Q	S	C	W	C
D	N	T	Y	Q	E	U	V	O	T	P	T	C	O	S	V	E	T	F	F
X	T	A	A	X	N	K	S	H	T	I	M	L	T	U	O	I	B	V	B
O	F	L	L	N	T	O	F	S	X	A	C	D	Q	I	S	B	N	H	R
V	L	T	N	H	I	G	R	M	I	A	O	P	O	Y	V	J	H	G	L
C	H	P	V	L	V	J	V	Q	E	R	M	L	H	I	V	E	O	Z	C
D	R	L	A	T	E	A	Z	C	C	O	N	S	I	D	E	R	A	T	E

Thankful for Our Friends

Name: ______________________

A good way to make a friendship stronger is to let your friend know why you are thankful for him or her.

Answer the questions.

1. What is your friend's name or nickname?

____

2. How long have you been friends?

____

3. What do you like to do together?

____

____

4. What is it about your friend that makes you thankful to have him or her as a friend?

____

____

5. How do you let your friend know that you care?

____

____

Compliments

Name: ______________________

A **compliment** is something kind that someone says to another person. Most people appreciate compliments.

Read the compliments inside the stars. Color the ones that state something that is true about you.

1.

Write the name of a person in each circle. Then write a compliment you would like to give that person in the matching circle.

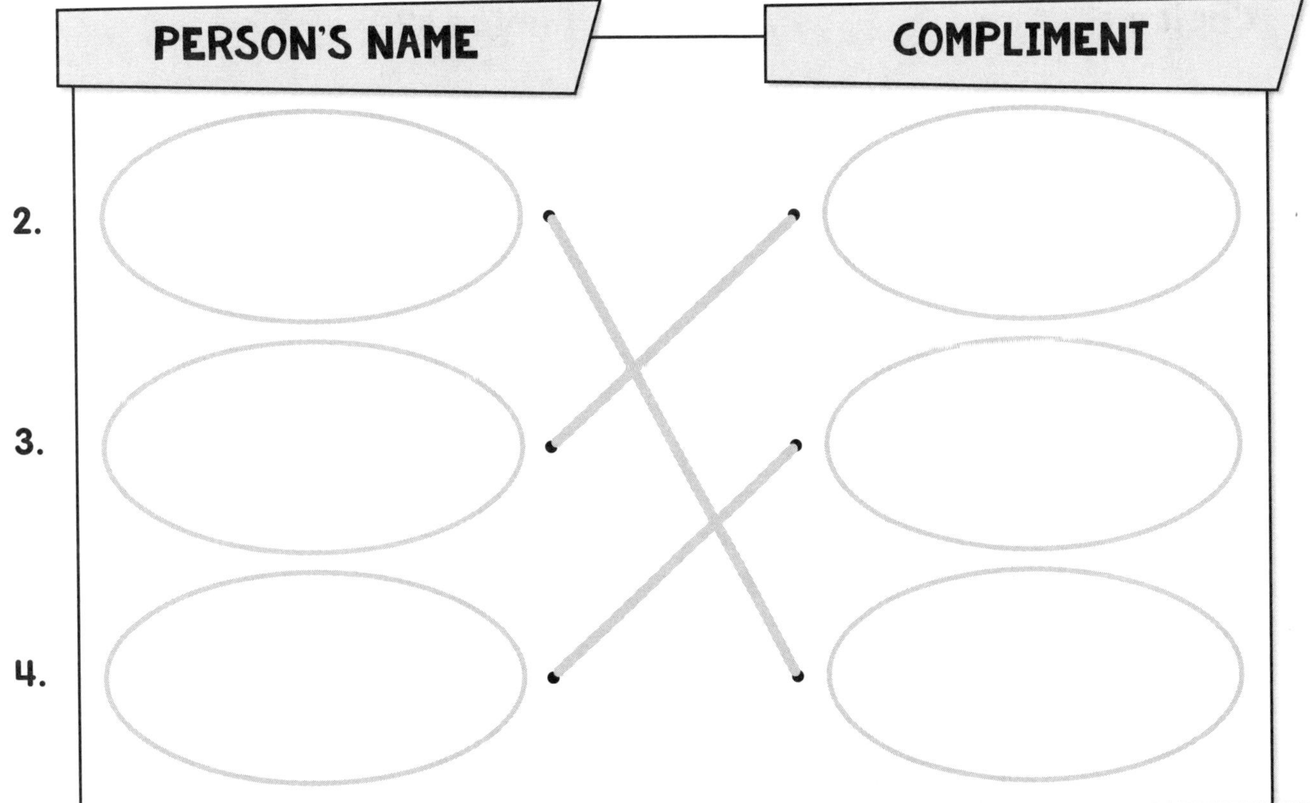

Choices Can Affect Relationships

Name: ______________________

Our choices can affect other people and our relationships with them. Think about all the possible outcomes before making a choice.

Read about the situation. Then answer the item.

Lanh wanted to have a sleepover at his house. His two best friends, Devon and Malik, weren't getting along, though. They had a fight a few days earlier. Devon asked Lanh to take his side against Malik. Then Malik tried to convince Lanh that Devon was totally wrong. Lanh was super nervous about inviting them both to his sleepover. "Which one should I invite?" he thought. "Maybe I shouldn't invite either of them." He didn't want to pick sides.

Write two different choices Lanh can make. For each choice you write, write one possible outcome.

Choice #1	**Choice #2**
Outcome #1	**Outcome #2**

Caring

Name: ____________________

In each circle, write one way that people show you they care about you.

Describe the ways that you show others you care about them.

Awkward Situations

Name: ____________________

Sometimes a situation is awkward. Awkward situations can be embarrassing or uncomfortable.

Think about a time when you had to deal with an awkward situation with another person. Draw a picture to show the situation. Then write to describe it in detail.

1.

____

____

____

____

Read about each situation below. Then color the number of emojis to rate how awkward you think it is. 1 = not awkward 5 = very awkward

2. At lunch, your classmates are talking about a birthday party they went to over the weekend. Everyone was at the party except you.

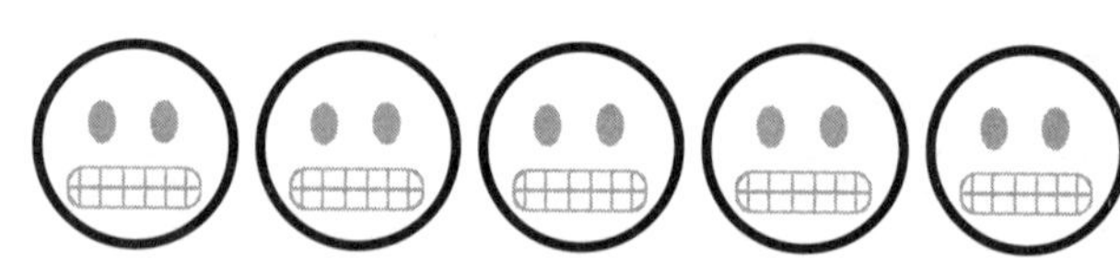

3. You accused your friend of lying to you in front of some of your other friends. Then you found out that you were wrong, and you have to say sorry.

We Can Disagree and Still Get Along

Name: ____________________

Sometimes a person says something that you don't agree with. When you practice **constructive disagreement**, you disagree in a respectful way.

Read.

Ruby's friends were complaining about school. Their teacher had given them a lot of math homework. Ruby shrugged. "I don't mind the homework," she said. "I love math."

Ruby's friends didn't agree with her opinion. Rate each of their responses on a scale of one to five stars. 1 = not constructive 5 = very constructive

1. "Really?" Cheng said. "I didn't think anyone liked math."

2. "My favorite is art," Omar said. "What do you like about math, Ruby?"

3. "Math stinks!" Samara said. "Science is better."

4. "I don't agree," Enrique said. "I like social studies more."

5. "People who like math are lame," said Chloe.

Because We Are Friends

Name: ____________________

The sentences below tell about friendship. Finish each sentence with a word. Write the word in the puzzle.

Down

1. We _____ each other.
3. I accept you, and you _____ me.
5. We treat each other like _____ members.

Across

2. We _____ honestly when we have a problem with each other.
4. We _____ to each other with our hearts, not just our ears.
6. It's like we are one _____.

Do This, Not That

Name: ______________________

Think about the things that a person should do to show respect to others. Color the hexagons that tell how to show respect to others.

Show kindness to others.

Listen to people when they are speaking to you.

Spend time with people you care about.

Say mean things about people behind their back.

Reply when people ask you a question.

Help people when they need your help.

Ignore people when you feel like it.

Each Person, Each Relationship

Name: ____________________________

Every person is unique. The relationships you have with people are special.

Think about what makes each relationship unique. Write about each one.

1. A sibling or cousin: ____________________________
   name

   ____

   ____

   ____

2. A friend: ____________________________
   name

   ____

   ____

   ____

3. A teacher: ____________________________
   name

   ____

   ____

   ____

SEL and Writing

Introduce SEL and writing to your students.

One way that we can let others know how we feel is to write our feelings. We can write an email or a letter. We can make a card. Or we can write a short message. Writing to communicate can be very different from speaking. When you speak, there is usually someone else who is also talking back to you. But with writing, you can take your time and choose your words carefully. You can write everything you want to say without anyone interrupting. Some people like to communicate through writing. But writing is not just for telling others how you feel or what you think. You can choose to write in a journal that only you will read. You can choose to write your own stories. You can write your own jokes. You can write your own songs or poems. Or you can just write and write and write, and it doesn't even have to make sense! When you write, you are free to write whatever you want. There are no rules or limits to what you can write. So write about anything at all, as long as you keep writing!

Topics covered in this unit:

Emotions	Inclusion	Mindfulness
Creativity	Body language	Empathy
Personal space	Communication	Acceptance
Manners	Cultural differences	Rules

Sibling Time

Name: ____________________

Read the story.

Martin was watching his six-year-old brother, James, after school. He wanted to make him a healthy snack before Mom got home from work.

"Hey, buddy," said Martin, "how about some yogurt and berries?"

"No, thanks. I had some trail mix," answered James, pointing to an open bag on the counter.

Martin picked up the bag and poured some trail mix onto the table. He read the ingredients: pecans, cranberries, raisins, sunflower seeds, chocolate chips.

"Hmm. James, all the chocolate chips are missing," said Martin. "What happened?"

Continue the story.

Better Choices

Name: ______________________

Think about a time when you reacted to something in a negative way, or in a way you're not happy about. Then write about it.

What happened?

How did it make you feel?

What could you do differently next time?

Challenging Times

Name: ______________________________

What is this boy doing? How does he feel? How can you tell? Write a story that describes how he arrived at this situation and what the outcome was.

Title: ______________________________

____

____

____

____

____

____

____

____

____

____

Forming an Opinion with Pros and Cons

Name: ______________________

A list of pros and cons is a tool that helps you analyze both sides of an issue. The pros are positives, or reasons to say yes. The cons are negatives, or reasons to say no.

Do you think children younger than 12 years of age should have social media accounts? Make a list of pros and cons to organize your thoughts.

PROS	CONS

Write your final opinion about the issue here:

____

____

____

____

____

____

Friendship Haiku

Name: ______________________________

A haiku is a poem with three lines that do not rhyme. The first line has five syllables, the second has seven, and the third has five.

Write a haiku about friendship. Use the examples as inspiration.

To be a good friend
Takes kindness and empathy
I am a good friend

Communication
Requires active listening
I hear you, my friend

Reaching a Goal with Grit

Name: ____________________

When we say a person has **grit**, we mean that person is willing to keep trying something even when it becomes difficult. People with grit can persevere. That means they don't give up.

Read the story about the adventurer Abu Taleb. Parts of the story are missing. In these parts, Abu needs grit. Write the missing parts to help Abu finish her quest.

Abu Taleb and the Crystal

Abu Taleb climbed up Mount Fear. She was searching for the Cave of Chaos. If the legends were true, the Crystal was in the cave. But the trail was steep. Abu's foot slipped on a loose rock, and she stumbled. She climbed back to her feet. When she looked up, her heart sank. The cave's entrance was still far above her. Her legs felt heavy. Abu thought about turning back...

____

____

____

Finally, Abu reached the cave's entrance. She took out a map of the cave. It showed a complex network of rooms and tunnels. She stepped inside. Deeper and deeper she walked, following the map. But soon she was surrounded by darkness. She couldn't see any details on the map. There was a chill in the air. Abu heard things moving all around her. She was terrified! Part of her wanted to turn around…

____

____

____

Reaching a Goal with Grit, continued

Name: ______________________

Abu's foot bumped something. It was an old piece of wood. She used it to make a torch. Now she could see where she was going! She checked her map again and quickly figured out where she was. She hurried down a long tunnel, expecting to reach a room. But instead, she hit a dead-end. Abu stomped her foot. She hurried down a different tunnel, but that brought her back to where she started! Abu got mad—and impatient. She ran faster and faster, trying to figure out where she was. Before long, Abu was totally lost! How would she ever find the Crystal?

____

____

____

Abu gasped when she stepped into the chamber. There it was: the Crystal! She gently lifted it off its pedestal. The chamber rumbled, but Abu didn't notice. She was gazing at the Crystal and thinking about how much it was worth. Then Abu sighed. It doesn't belong to me, Abu thought. She put it back on the pedestal. But it was too late. Abu had already set off a trap! Rocks fell all around her. Abu was still tired from everything she'd done that day. But now she had to get out of the cave—fast!

____

____

____

How Would It Feel?

Name: ______________________

Read each question. Then write a paragraph to answer it.

1. How would you feel if you suddenly had to leave your country to live in a different country where you had to learn a new language?

____

____

____

____

____

____

2. How would you feel if you were treated differently because your home looks different from the homes of your classmates?

____

____

____

____

____

____

Write an Acrostic Poem

Name: ______________________

An acrostic poem is a poem that has a word written from top to bottom. Each letter of the word begins a new line or sentence that is related to the word's meaning. Here is an example of an acrostic poem:

> **H**aving someone you care about welcome you with open arms.
> **U**nlike anything else in the world, in a good way.
> **G**reat when you're happy, sad, or somewhere in between.

Write an acrostic poem for the word *kindness*.

SEL and Reading

Introduce SEL and reading to your students.

When you read, you get to learn about a character's experience, or what a character is going through. Fictional characters often have the same problems that people have in real life. That's why we can learn from both fiction and nonfiction stories. We can learn how characters deal with problems and how their choices affect others. We can learn about the kinds of feelings that characters or real people have. Reading can also help us learn about different cultures, different families, and life in different places. We can imagine the characters' lives and think about how our own lives are different and the same. Trying to understand how a character feels helps some people to better understand how people in the real world feel. When you read, think about the story and see if you can take away a message or lesson that can help you in your life.

Topics covered in this unit:

Creativity	Making friends	Mindfulness
Strengths and weaknesses	Body language	Empathy
Bravery	Communication	Acceptance
Microaggressions	Civility	Life lessons

A Different World

Name: ______________________

Read the story.

It was the year 2090, and Tyreeka and her dad drove their rover along the rocky Mars trail. Tyreeka's family was one of the first ones to move to Mars from Earth. It felt scary sometimes, because people were still learning about Mars. There were very few people there compared to Earth. And there was also the possibility of running into Martians. But nobody was sure if there were Martians. "Just think, Tyreeka," her dad said. "What if there really are Martians and we meet one someday? What will you say? What will you do?"

Tyreeka had never thought about it before. A Martian was bound to be super different from an Earth person, right? "If we met some Martians, I don't think I'd be very friendly, at least not at first," Tyreeka said. "They'd be too different."

"But just because they're different, why does that mean you shouldn't be friendly?" asked her dad. "Wouldn't it be good to be friendly and show them you are kind?"

Imagine that you are in Tyreeka's situation, and you are meeting a Martian for the first time. Draw a picture of yourself and the Martian, and show how you would treat the Martian.

Zaldar, the Not-Totally-Perfect Knight

Name: ____________________

We all have strengths and weaknesses. When we recognize what our strengths and weaknesses are, we can reach our goals. We can use our strengths and work on improving our weaknesses.

Read the story.

A wizard hid the queen's gold in a maze. Two knights, Glinn and Zaldar, entered the maze to find it. At one point, they could either turn left or right. Glinn wanted to turn right. But Zaldar had studied a map of the maze. He knew which way to go.

"That's a dumb idea, Glinn," Zaldar said. "We need to turn left."

Glinn got mad, and they argued. Finally, Zaldar stomped off to the left. Glinn went to the right and soon got lost. He wound up back where he'd started. Zaldar found an iron door. Peeking through a hole, he saw the gold. "Yes!" He tried to push the door open, but it was too heavy for one person to push. Luckily, he found an iron bar. Using it as a lever, he moved the door—just a bit. "Grr!" Zaldar used all of his strength. Finally, the door was open. He hurried into the room without looking. A troll grabbed him! Zaldar screamed and broke free of the troll's grip. Glinn heard Zaldar and ran into the room. Together, he and Zaldar fought off the troll. Then they gathered the gold and returned it to the queen.

What are Zaldar's strengths and weaknesses? List two in the boxes below.

Strengths	Weaknesses

The Race

Name: ______________________

When people feel **empathy** for someone, they feel the way that person feels. They understand what the person is going through and might feel as if they're going through it, too.

Read the story.

The race started, and Zeke, Hazeema, and Sasha started running. The crowd cheered. Right away, Hazeema's father had a big smile. He threw his hands in the air and waved them around. Sasha's mom cheered, but she was frowning and biting her lip. Suddenly Zeke's mom cringed as if she'd just gotten hurt. She hurried down the steps to get closer to the track. Then she wiped her brow and continued to cheer on her son. Just then Sasha's mom stood up and whistled. As she jumped up and down, Hazeema's father's eyes went wide. He cheered for Hazeema, but his shoulders slumped a bit. Finally, the race ended. Everyone clapped and cheered.

Answer the items about the story.

1. The parents in the crowd showed empathy during the race. Use their reactions to infer who came in first, second, and third place, and write the names on the lines below.

______________________	______________________	______________________
first place	second place	third place

2. Why do you think the parents empathized with their kids during the race?

____

____

____

Read the Adage

Name: ______________________

An **adage** is a saying. It states an idea that many people consider to be true or think of as "common knowledge."

Read the adage. Then draw a line to match it to its literal meaning.

Adage	Literal Meaning
Birds of a feather flock together. 	People who are very different sometimes like each other's differences and become friends.
Opposites attract. 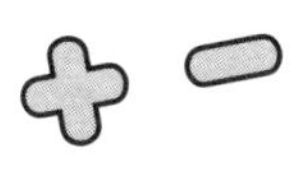	People who arrive early or prepare ahead of time get more than people who do not.
Better late than never. 	If you don't know about something, then you cannot worry about it or have hurt feelings about it.
The early bird gets the worm.	People who have similarities sometimes become friends.
What you don't know can't hurt you.	It's better to take care of your responsibilities late than not at all.

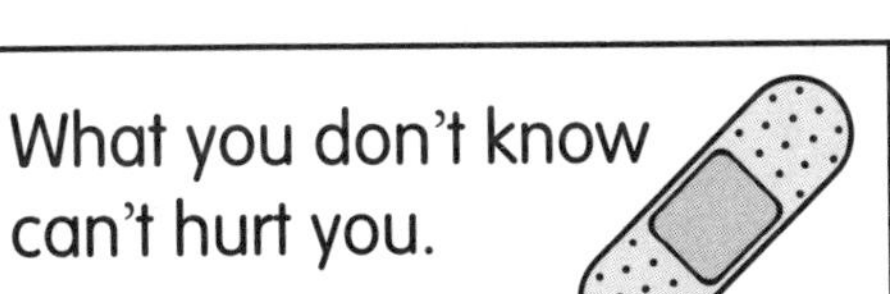

Microaggressions

Name: ______________________

A **microaggression** is a statement that is brief but hurtful. It shows a general negative attitude or idea about a group of people. Because microaggressions happen so quickly, they often take people off guard. Sometimes people say microaggressions without meaning to, but the statements can still be hurtful.

Read each microaggression. Then write to explain why each microaggression could be hurtful in some people's opinions.

1. Whoa, your name is Arundhati? That's hard to say! I don't think I'm going to be able to pronounce that. Can I just use a nickname for you? Can I call you Arun?

____

____

2. It's interesting that your parents immigrated here from another country. So, are you a citizen here?

____

____

3. You would be so pretty if only your hair were a little bit less wild and curly.

____

____

4. Well, I know you're not really asking my opinion, but I don't think people will want to hear about your family's culture. Maybe you should pick a different topic for your speech, one that more people in your class will find interesting.

____

____

Name: ____________________

In the conversation below, the microaggression statements are in the gray speech bubbles. Read the conversation. Then answer the items.

1. Do you think the woman was trying to be rude or hurtful to the girl? Write **yes** or **no**. ____________

2. Do you think the things the woman said could be hurtful to some people? ____________

   Explain your answer.

   ____

   ____

Is It Polite?

Name: ______________________

Read each comment. Tell whether you think the comment is polite or impolite. Then write to explain your opinion.

1. I was surprised when I met your mom. I thought she would look different. She is so pretty. You look nothing like her.

○ polite ○ impolite

____

____

____

2. I know you haven't asked for my opinion, but I thought I'd share what I think anyway. I've noticed that you bring a lot of junk food for your lunch every day, and you never bring fruits or vegetables. Do you really think that's a good idea?

○ polite ○ impolite

____

____

____

3. How do you like those shoes you're wearing? I saw those same shoes at the store, and I didn't like them. The color is so ugly. I hope they're comfortable.

○ polite ○ impolite

____

____

____

Would You Send This Email?

Name: ____________________

Read each email. Then write an **X** to tell if you would send it or if you would rather find a nicer way to say what the email is trying to say.

1.

New Message

To: The Owner of Buy Smart Mart
From: Your Customer
Subject: Broken video game

Hello,

I am writing to say that I will never shop at your store again. The video game I bought there was broken when I opened it. Your store is the worst store I have ever been to. The people who work at your store are awful.

-Your Angry Customer

SEND

❑ I would send the email. ❑ I would rather find a nicer way to say this.

2.

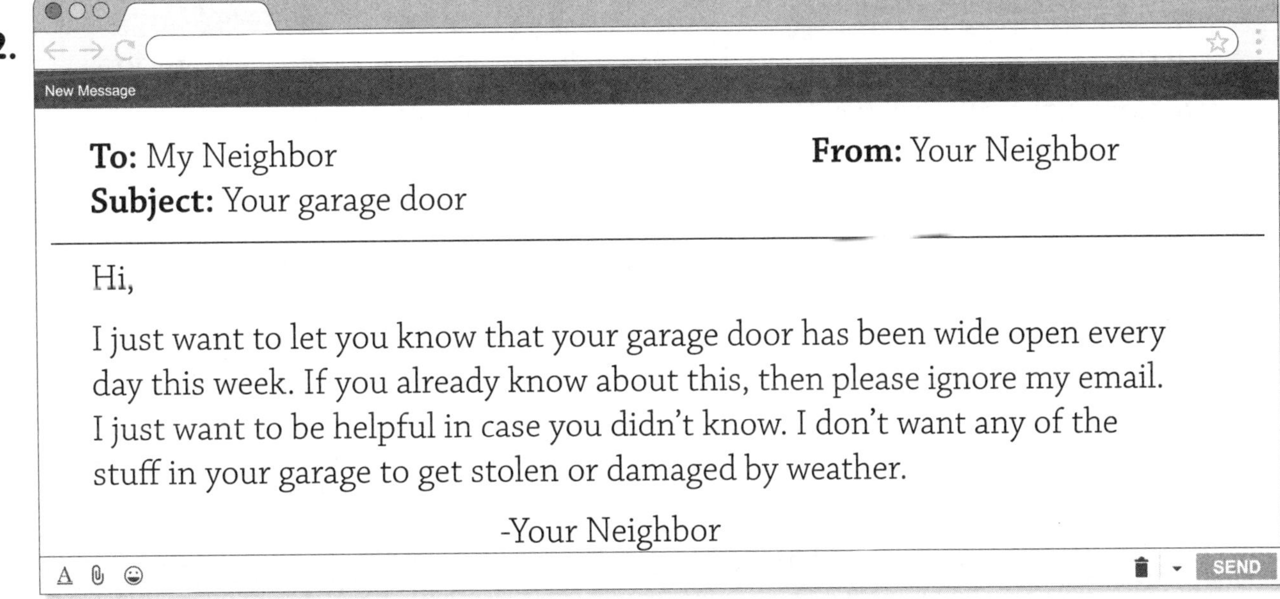

New Message

To: My Neighbor
From: Your Neighbor
Subject: Your garage door

Hi,

I just want to let you know that your garage door has been wide open every day this week. If you already know about this, then please ignore my email. I just want to be helpful in case you didn't know. I don't want any of the stuff in your garage to get stolen or damaged by weather.

-Your Neighbor

SEND

❑ I would send the email. ❑ I would rather find a nicer way to say this.

Read Proverbs

Name: ____________________

A **proverb** is a common saying that gives advice.

Read the proverb. Then draw a line to match it to its literal meaning.

Proverb	Literal Meaning
Don't bite off more than you can chew. •	• Do not create problems where there are no problems, and do not bring up old problems that have been solved already.
Don't judge a book by its cover. •	• Be cautious before making an important decision.
Look before you leap. •	• Do not make assumptions about other people when you do not know them or their experiences.
Learn to walk before you run. •	• Do not take on more responsibilities and work than you can safely handle.
Let sleeping dogs lie. •	• Learn the basics before you take on more difficult tasks so that you are confident rather than arrogant.

SEL and Math

Introduce SEL and math to your students.

Some people like doing math, and some people don't. It's okay to like or not like math. Even if you don't like it, math is still an important skill. Some people don't like math because they think they are not good at it. No person is good at everything, and it is okay to make mistakes. Just remember that you can improve at anything if you keep trying and keep practicing. And if you keep trying to do math, you might even find that you actually like it!

Topics covered in this unit:

Self-care	Mindfulness	Financial responsibility
Cooperation	Time perception	Comfort

Reward!

Name: ______________________

People often give a reward for help returning something that was lost. Sometimes parents offer their children money as a reward for good behavior or good grades. Even getting paid for a job is considered a reward. How do rewards affect what you do?

Read the story and look at the flyer. Then write whether the reward is enough for you to choose to help. Explain your answer.

Lost Dog!

Our dog, Spike, dug out of our yard on Apex Avenue. He is 7 years old, deaf, and not wearing a collar.

- Tan color
- Missing Dec. 15
- Call 555-6326
- $10 reward!

1. A family in your neighborhood is looking for their lost dog. Would you help look for this dog and return it to the family? Explain your answer.

____

____

2. Imagine that your parents want you to be a doctor some day. They want you to take advanced science classes now in a special online program. They will pay you $50 for each class you pass. Would you take them? Explain your answer.

____

____

3. A new neighbor just moved in. He is looking for someone to help clean up his basement. It is full of spider webs. Also, it flooded once, so there is mud and debris covering the floor. Would you take the job? Explain your answer.

____

____

Help Wanted!

Clean out my dirty basement.

- Shovel mud
- Get rid of spider webs
- Will pay $65
- Call 555-4259

A New Way to Look at a Problem

Name: ______________________________

When we have a problem, we might feel upset or let down. But sometimes problems can help us learn. We can try to look at problems as lessons that we can learn from. Have you ever thought, "This is too hard for me"? You might choose to look at this problem another way and see if it helps you feel better.

Solve the math problems. Then find each answer beneath the lines below. Write the letters on the lines to spell out a message.

A	C	D	E
$6\overline{)82.8}$	$4\overline{)98.4}$	$5\overline{)92.0}$	$9\overline{)96.3}$

F	H	M	O
$8\overline{)287.2}$	$2\overline{)123.0}$	$7\overline{)280.7}$	$6\overline{)325.8}$

R	S	U	Y
$3\overline{)14.76}$	$5\overline{)46.85}$	$8\overline{)64.64}$	$4\overline{)29.00}$

___ ___ ___ ___ ___
4.92 10.7 13.8 24.6 61.5

___ ___ ___
35.9 54.3 4.92

___ ___ ___ ___
7.25 54.3 8.08 4.92

___ ___ ___ ___ ___ ___
18.4 4.92 10.7 13.8 40.1 9.37

How Do You Rate?

Name: ____________________

When we rate something, we give it a value on a number scale, such as from 1 to 5. People rate places they eat, items they buy, and services they receive. Ratings can be used to see where improvements can be made.

Read each statement about yourself. Then circle the rating you give yourself, using a scale from 1 to 5. Explain your rating.

1. When something bad happens, I think before I react.

1	2	3	4	5
never	occasionally	sometimes	usually	almost always

Explain. ____________________

2. When I disagree with someone, I listen to the other person's point of view.

1	2	3	4	5
never	occasionally	sometimes	usually	almost always

Explain. ____________________

3. When I make a decision, I accept responsibility and credit for what happens.

1	2	3	4	5
never	occasionally	sometimes	usually	almost always

Explain. ____________________

Add up the three ratings. Now divide by 3. This is your average rating: ______

Let's Work Together

Name: ______________________

Working together adds fun, subtracts boredom, multiplies productivity, and divides large, difficult tasks into small, easy steps.

Four neighbors work together in their community garden. Read about how they share the load. Then answer the questions.

1. Neera is planting 6 tomato plants every hour.

   In 2½ hours, how many tomato plants are in the ground? ______________________

2. Ahmed is watering each row of the garden. He spends 8 minutes on each row. It takes him from 10:30 to 12:02 to water every row.

   How many rows does he water? ______________________

   After watering, Ahmed spends an hour picking 27 ripe apples. He leaves 18 on the tree to continue ripening.

   What fraction of the apples were ripe? ______________________

3. Tanya and Felipe are weeding the potted plants. They start at opposite corners of the garden and work toward the center. After 2.4 hours, they meet in the middle. Tanya has weeded 16 pots. Felipe has weeded 1.25 times as many.

   How many pots did Felipe weed? ______________________

   How many pots did they weed in all? ______________________

   To find the average time it took to weed a pot, divide the number of minutes they worked by the total number of pots they weeded.

   What was the average time to weed a pot? ______________________

Healthy Heart Math

Name: ______________________

There are many measurements that help us know if we are healthy. Some can even show how we are feeling. How fast your heart beats is one of those measurements.

The speed of your heartbeat is called your pulse. You can feel your pulse in several places. You can press your hand over your heart. You can press your neck just above the left collarbone. You can press just under your left wrist. Figure out which place is easiest for you to find your pulse. Practice counting heartbeats.

For this activity, use a timer or have your teacher or a partner time you for 15 seconds. Find your pulse before starting. During the 15 seconds, count how many times your heart beats. Record the number in the table below. Do this in the following situations:

- after sitting quietly for several minutes
- after talking in a conversation or class discussion
- right after hearing a surprising noise
- after walking back to your room following lunch or a bathroom break
- right after running, playing a sport, or another form of exercise

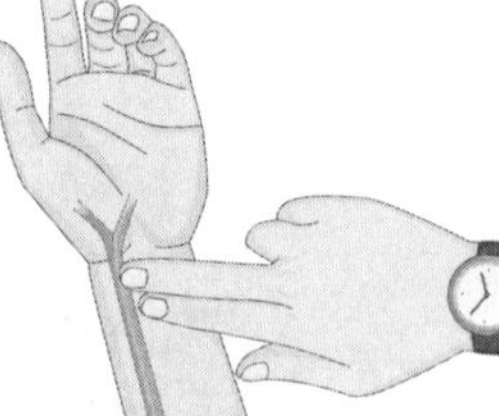

Record your data in the first row. Multiply each count by 4. Write the number in the last row.

	sitting	talking	surprised	walking	exercising
beats/15 seconds					
	x 4	x 4	x 4	x 4	x 4
beats/minute					

Write one thing that might cause your heart rate to rise. ______________________

Write one thing that might cause your heart rate to slow. ______________________

Budget Pie

Name: ______________________________

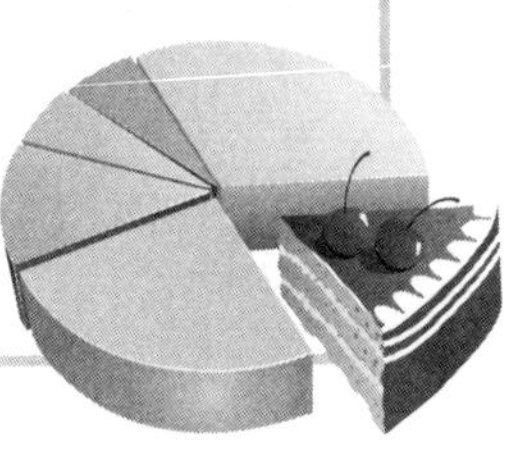

Pie can be cut into slices of different sizes. Big slices are fun to eat, but you don't get many. You can feed more people with smaller slices. Budgets work the same way. How you slice your money is up to you.

The table lists things that many students spend money on. Imagine you were given $100 to spend on these things. Decide how much of the $100 you would want to spend on each thing and write the amount in the table. You can also save some money for later to buy something in the future. You can leave some spaces blank, but the amounts should add up to 100.

Snacks	
Apps/music downloads	
Movies	
Video games	
Books/magazines	
Hobby equipment	

Clothes/footwear/ accessories	
Amusement parks	
Concerts/games	
Beauty/ hair products	
Gifts	
Savings	

Now use the numbers to make a pie graph. Label each piece of the pie graph.

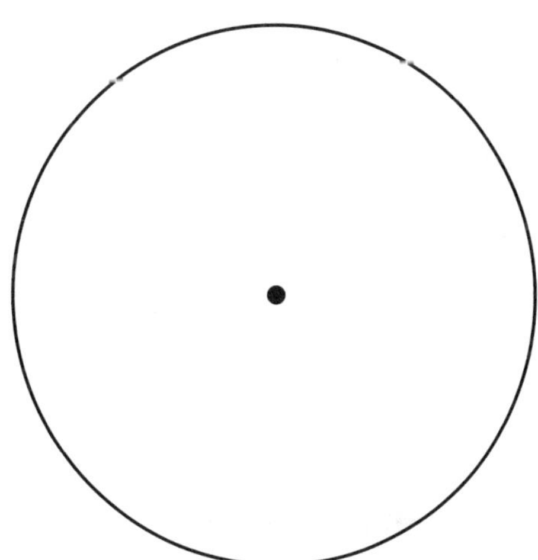

Time to Feel

Name: ____________________

Time perception is our sense of how long something lasts. An hour-long dentist appointment may feel like forever, but a long visit with your best friend may feel like ten minutes. It depends a lot on how we feel while doing different things.

Find a partner to do this activity. Have a stopwatch or a watch with a second hand available. Decide who will be Partner 1 and Partner 2. Then do each activity.

1. **Partner 1** When your partner says "go," smile as big as you can. Hold it until your partner tells you to stop. Your partner will time how long you smiled. Write down how much time you think passed. Then write down the actual time that your partner tells you.

____________________ ____________________

time estimate **actual time**

Partner 2 Now it's your turn to smile big while your partner times it.

____________________ ____________________

time estimate **actual time**

2. **Partner 1** When your partner says "go," frown sadly! Hold it until your partner tells you to stop. Write down how much time you think passed. Then write down the actual time that your partner tells you.

____________________ ____________________

time estimate **actual time**

Partner 2 Now it's your turn to frown when your partner says "go," and your partner will time you. Write down your estimate and the actual time for how long you frowned.

____________________ ____________________

time estimate **actual time**

Arrange Your Room

Name: ______________________

Everyone has the right to be comfortable. Different things give us comfort. Imagine that you have the furniture below and are moving into a new home. Arrange your furniture the way you want it. Just make sure it all fits inside.

Cut out the furniture pieces on this page. Arrange them in the room diagram on the next page. Glue or tape them in place when you decide where they will go. Color your furniture the way you want it to look.

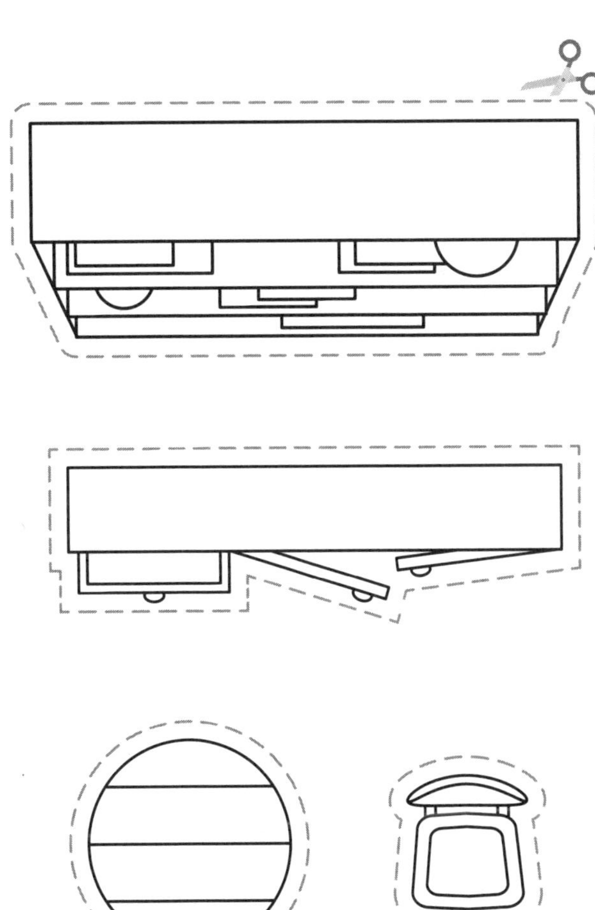

Arrange Your Room, continued

Name: ____________________

Closet Door

Window

Door

Window

SEL and Social Studies

Introduce SEL and social studies to your students.

All people are different in a lot of ways. But all people are the same in so many ways, too. Social studies helps us learn about people, all kinds of people. We can learn about people who may look different than we do or speak a different language. We can learn about people who live in different places or who do things differently than we do. Social studies lets us learn about how people did things a long time ago. It also teaches us about the kinds of food, music, clothing, and holidays that are in people's lives all around the world. Most importantly, social studies helps us learn about the problems that people have all around the world. We can learn about the problems people had in the past. And we can see how people come together to form a community and work together. The more we learn about other people, the better we can understand how we are all different and the same.

Topics covered in this unit:

Conflict resolution	Mindfulness	Self-awareness
Fear	Self-talk	Empathy

Trouble in Paradise

Name: ______________________________

If a disagreement or argument is serious enough, it's called a **conflict**. Conflicts can occur between individuals or entire societies. They can be simple arguments over what to watch on TV. Or they can be much more complicated, like a war. **Conflict resolution** occurs when people try to solve a problem peacefully.

Read the story. Then answer the question.

Four people were sailing far out to sea. One night, they got caught in a huge storm. Wind howled as waves crashed. The boat was thrown into some rocks. When the storm passed, the people climbed out of the boat. They were on a remote island.

"At least the island is nice," one person said. "It's like a tropical paradise!"

They didn't know when—or if—they'd be rescued. Everyone headed off in different directions to find food, water, and shelter. Later, they met back up at the wrecked boat. One person had found a freshwater spring. Another person had found a grove of banana trees. A third person had found the perfect beach for fishing. The fourth person hadn't found anything in particular, but she knew how to build a shelter.

"The freshwater spring is mine," the first person said. "I found it."

The second person frowned. "Then I own the banana grove!"

"I'm willing to share my beach," the third person said. "But only if you two share the things you found."

Just then, rain started to fall. The fourth person started to build a shelter. "This is just for me!" she said.

What is the conflict in the story?

____

____

Trouble in Paradise,
continued

Name: ______________________________

The people on the island don't know if they'll be rescued. So for now, they have to form their own society. But they already have a conflict. There are a variety of ways this conflict can be resolved.

Think of two possible resolutions for this conflict. Describe them.

Resolution #1	Resolution #2

For each resolution, read the question and circle the answer.

Resolution 1:	Solves the problem?	Yes	No	Maybe
Resolution 2:	Solves the problem?	Yes	No	Maybe
Resolution 1:	Makes everyone happy?	Yes	No	Maybe
Resolution 2:	Makes everyone happy?	Yes	No	Maybe
Resolution 1:	Treats everyone fairly?	Yes	No	Maybe
Resolution 2:	Treats everyone fairly?	Yes	No	Maybe

Trouble in Paradise,
continued

Name: ______________________

When trying to resolve a conflict, you need to think about the people who are arguing. What do they want? Will your resolution make everyone happy? Will anyone feel like they're being treated unfairly?

Pick the resolution that you think will work best for the people on the island. Then imagine that you have to get them to follow your advice. Write a speech that convinces them to agree with your resolution.

How I'd Help My Community

Name: ____________________

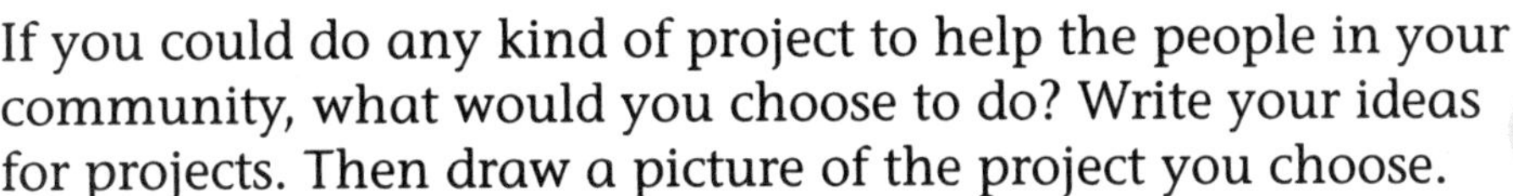

Sometimes people plant a tree to honor the memory of a person they cared for. Sometimes people start a vegetable garden to help grow food for their community.

If you could do any kind of project to help the people in your community, what would you choose to do? Write your ideas for projects. Then draw a picture of the project you choose.

My Project

Cultural Fusions

Name: ____________________

Sometimes a culture borrows things from other cultures, such as clothing styles or food flavors. This can create something new, which is a cultural fusion.

Draw or write about one fusion that you have seen or experienced for each category.

Music

Example:

Arabic hip hop songs

Food

Example:

Korean tacos

Clothing

Example:

Australian bush hat

That's Not Fair!

Name: ____________________

When a group of people is treated unfairly based on a characteristic like the color of their skin or their gender, that treatment is a **social injustice**.

List three instances of social injustice that you know of.

1.	**2.**	**3.**

List three ways to promote social justice.

1.	**2.**	**3.**

Use Your Voice

A Visit to Queens

Name: ______________________

Read the story. Then answer the items about the story on page 105.

Lisa's first visit to her cousin Debbie's house was something she would never forget. Debbie lived in an apartment in Queens, New York. As Lisa and her parents pulled up in a taxi, Debbie and her parents were waiting outside on their busy sidewalk to greet them. Debbie ran up to the taxi door, flung it open, and said, "C'mon, let's go play!" The next thing Lisa knew, they were running down the block.

"Slow down," Lisa said as she twisted her neck to see inside the store that had large Chinese characters printed on the window. "Where are we going?"

"We are going to Samira's house first," said Debbie. As Lisa climbed the stairs to the apartment building and followed Debbie down the noisy, aromatic hallway, she heard at least two different languages coming from the apartment doors. She passed small children playing a game she did not recognize. She saw a tall dark-complected woman who wore a colorful wrap on her head and a long multi-colored dress.

As they approached Samira's door, Debbie said, "Samira's family is Arab. Her mom always makes the most delicious food, so don't be shy."

Samira greeted them with a big smile and invited them in. Lisa couldn't help but look around with fascination. The apartment featured multi-colored lights of different sizes hanging from the ceiling, colorful rugs on the floor, and a long table covered with food and surrounded by people. Samira introduced Lisa to her parents and her many aunts and uncles. They greeted her warmly. Samira's mom said, "Samira tells us you are here all the way from Montana. How do you like Queens so far?" Lisa looked around the room at the interesting food, clothes, and decorations.

"I love Queens," answered Lisa. "And I love your home. By the way, Debbie told me not to be shy. I didn't eat anything on the plane," she said, eyeing the food on the table. Samira's dad chuckled and said, "Did you hear that, Amira? Another person is here to bring you joy by eating your food!" Before Lisa knew it, she was at the table with a plate of foods she had never seen before. Debbie and Samira sat down, too, and as they all ate, Lisa couldn't wait to find out who they were visiting next.

A Visit to Queens, continued

Name: ______________________

Answer the items about the story you read.

1. Based on the story, what can you infer about Queens, New York?

____

____

2. Lisa saw, heard, and smelled many things that she was not familiar with in Queens. She reacted positively to these things. How might you react to these things if you were in her situation?

____

____

3. Do you agree or disagree that "A Different World" would also be a good title for this story? Explain your opinion.

____

____

4. Draw a picture of something that was described in the story.

Cultural Differences

Name: ___________________________

People from different cultures eat different foods, have different celebrations, dress differently, and speak differently. Many people try to show respect for cultural differences.

Draw a line to match the disrespectful situation to a response that shows respect.

Situation			You Show Respect by Saying
You hear two kids speaking a different language. The kids beside them are imitating them in a mean way.	•	•	"I haven't seen that food before. I bet it tastes good. What is it called?"
You see a girl eating food that looks strange to you. It also smells funny to you.	•	•	"People have all types of skin color and hair texture. It's a natural part of being human."
You see a boy who has a different skin color than you and a different texture of hair. Other kids are making fun of how he looks.	•	•	"You speak one language and they speak another. It's nothing to make fun of or laugh about."

Thinking About My Background

Name: ______________________

Read each item. Think about your answer carefully, and then write it on the lines.

1. What is your **nationality**? Your nationality is the country that you call home. It is the country you are a citizen of or the country where you live. You can have more than one nationality.

____
____
____
____

2. What **ethnicity** do you identify with, or what groups do you belong to? Your ethnicity is the culture, values, and beliefs of a group that you belong to. You can have more than one ethnicity. We often get our ethnicity from our parents or family. We can also join or choose to identify with an ethnic group.

____
____
____
____

3. What are some parts of your **culture**? Many things make up a culture. Customs, food, clothing, art, architecture, writing, music, and other things are part of culture. Culture is how a group of people live and interact. Many things can shape the culture of a group, such as the country they live in or the social interests they have.

____
____
____
____

Where in the World?

Name: ______________________

Color the shape if it names a country you are curious about.

Switzerland	Mexico	Pakistan	New Zealand
Netherlands	Spain	United States of America	Japan
Thailand	Brazil	Jordan	Australia
Canada	Ireland	Vietnam	Ethiopia
El Salvador	Portugal	Namibia	Laos
China	Afghanistan	Singapore	Greece

Customs and Habits

Name: ______________________

Different people have different customs and habits. Some of our customs and habits help us feel like we belong. Sometimes they help us feel happy or healthy.

Read the list of customs and habits. Color ☺ next to the ones that you like to do or that you would like to start doing.

Color ☹ next to the ones that you do not like to do or would not like to start doing.

1. Eating meals with other people ☺ ☹

2. Sleeping over at a friend's house ☺ ☹

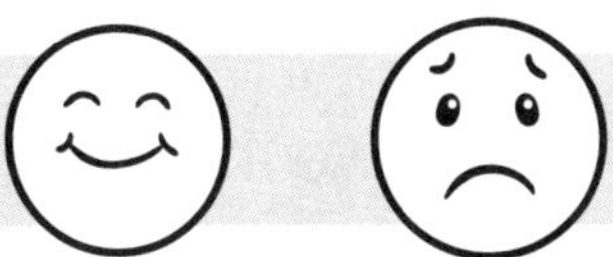

3. Having a family pet ☺ ☹

4. Going camping ☺ ☹

5. Watching a movie in your car at a drive-in theater ☺ ☹

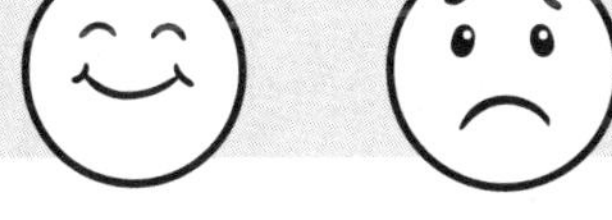

6. Having rice at breakfast ☺ ☹

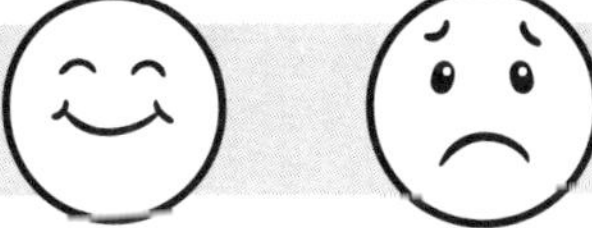

7. Using chopsticks ☺ ☹

8. Eating breakfast foods for dinner ☺ ☹

9. Eating popcorn when you watch a movie ☺ ☹

What I Think

Name: ____________________

Write a word or phrase to finish each sentence and share your opinion.

1. I think that all people feel ____________________ sometimes.

2. I think that people in every country are the same in this way:

____

____________________.

3. I believe that how people look is not as important as how they ____________

____

____________________.

4. I think it is ____________________ when people of different races, ethnicities, and nationalities are friends with each other.

5. I think that one of the best things that humans do for one another is this:

____

____________________.

Answer Key

Many of the activities in this book are not included in the answer key because answers vary based on each student's perspective and life experience.

Page 23

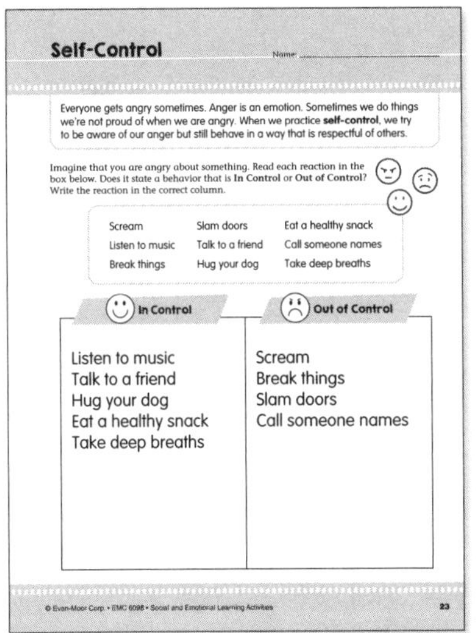

Self-Control Name: ______

Everyone gets angry sometimes. Anger is an emotion. Sometimes we do things we're not proud of when we are angry. When we practice **self-control**, we try to be aware of our anger but still behave in a way that is respectful of others.

Imagine that you are angry about something. Read each reaction in the box below. Does it state a behavior that is **In Control** or **Out of Control**? Write the reaction in the correct column.

Scream / Slam doors / Eat a healthy snack
Listen to music / Talk to a friend / Call someone names
Break things / Hug your dog / Take deep breaths

In Control	Out of Control
Listen to music	Scream
Talk to a friend	Break things
Hug your dog	Slam doors
Eat a healthy snack	Call someone names
Take deep breaths	

© Evan-Moor Corp. • EMC 6098 • Social and Emotional Learning Activities 23

Page 28

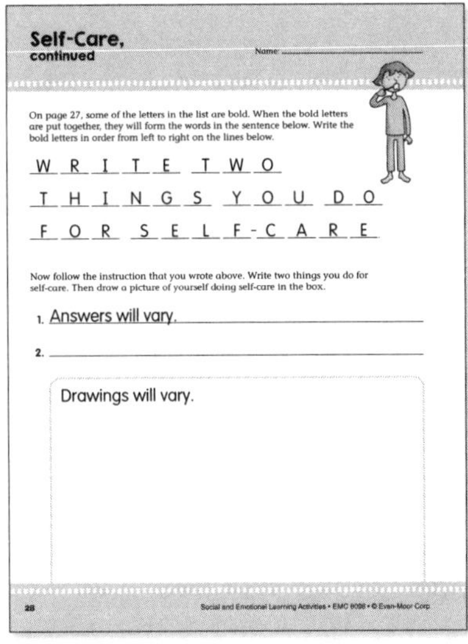

Self-Care, continued Name: ______

On page 27, some of the letters in the list are bold. When the bold letters are put together, they will form the words in the sentence below. Write the bold letters in order from left to right on the lines below.

W R I T E T W O
T H I N G S Y O U D O
F O R S E L F - C A R E

Now follow the instruction that you wrote above. Write two things you do for self-care. Then draw a picture of yourself doing self-care in the box.

1. Answers will vary.
2. ______

Drawings will vary.

28 Social and Emotional Learning Activities • EMC 6098 • © Evan-Moor Corp.

Page 36

Social Cues Name: ______

Finish each sentence. Write the word in the crossword.

Crossword answers: 1 EYES, 2 SHAKE, 3 LANGUAGE, 4 QUIET, 5 HAPPINESS, 6 HUG, 7 SURPRISE, 8 ANGER

Down
1. When people are annoyed, they roll their ______.
2. When you ______ your head, it means "no."
3. Social cues include body ______.
4. A finger to the lips says, "Be ______."

Across
5. A smile may signal ______.
6. A synonym of "embrace" is ______.
7. Raised eyebrows signal ______.
8. Crossed arms together with a frown could possibly signal ______.

36 Social and Emotional Learning Activities • EMC 6098 • © Evan-Moor Corp.

Page 41

Okay and Not Okay Name: ______

We all have opinions. It is okay to state your opinions, even if you disagree with others. But it is not okay to be disrespectful or to say things that are unkind and **uninformed**, or not based on facts.

Read the comment. Then color the circle to tell whether the comment is **okay** or **not okay** to say.

1. All people from that ethnic group have big noses. — not okay
2. Well, everyone has their own unique style of speaking. — okay
3. You know, she is probably very lazy. All people who look like she does are lazy. — not okay
4. Every person's body is different. The world is made up of different body types! — okay

© Evan-Moor Corp. • EMC 6098 • Social and Emotional Learning Activities 41

Page 57

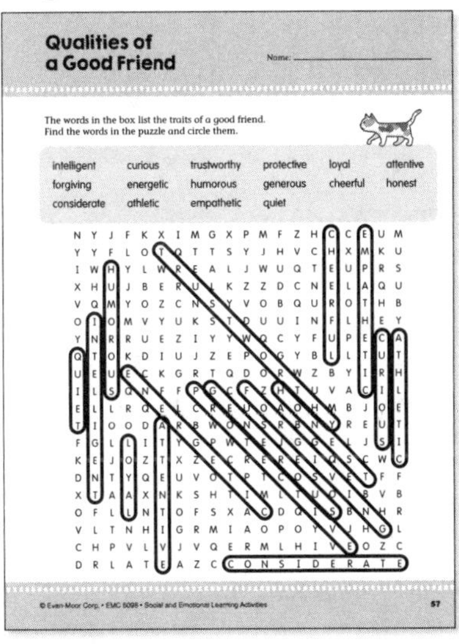

Qualities of a Good Friend Name: ______

The words in the box list the traits of a good friend. Find the words in the puzzle and circle them.

intelligent, curious, trustworthy, protective, loyal, attentive, forgiving, energetic, humorous, generous, cheerful, honest, considerate, athletic, empathetic, quiet

© Evan-Moor Corp. • EMC 6098 • Social and Emotional Learning Activities 57

Page 64

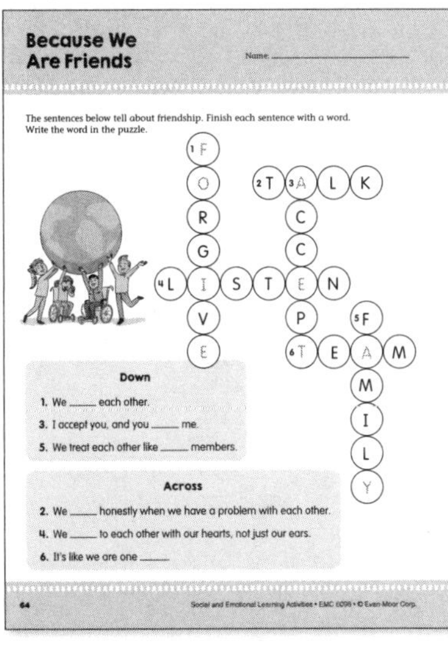

Because We Are Friends Name: ______

The sentences below tell about friendship. Finish each sentence with a word. Write the word in the puzzle.

Puzzle answers: 1 FORGIVE, 2 TALK, 3 ACCEPT, 4 LISTEN, 5 FAMILY, 6 TEAM

Down
1. We ______ each other.
3. I accept you, and you ______ me.
5. We treat each other like ______ members.

Across
2. We ______ honestly when we have a problem with each other.
4. We ______ to each other with our hearts, not just our ears.
6. It's like we are one ______.

64 Social and Emotional Learning Activities • EMC 6098 • © Evan-Moor Corp.

Page 65

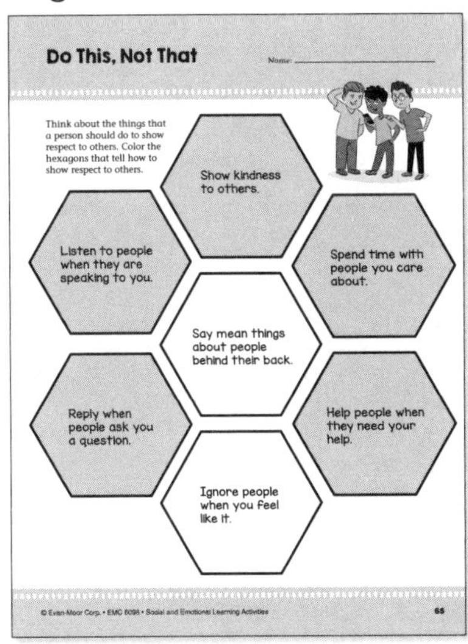

Do This, Not That Name: ______

Think about the things that a person should do to show respect to others. Color the hexagons that tell how to show respect to others.

Show kindness to others.
Listen to people when they are speaking to you.
Spend time with people you care about.
Say mean things about people behind their back.
Reply when people ask you a question.
Help people when they need your help.
Ignore people when you feel like it.

© Evan-Moor Corp. • EMC 6098 • Social and Emotional Learning Activities 65

Page 80

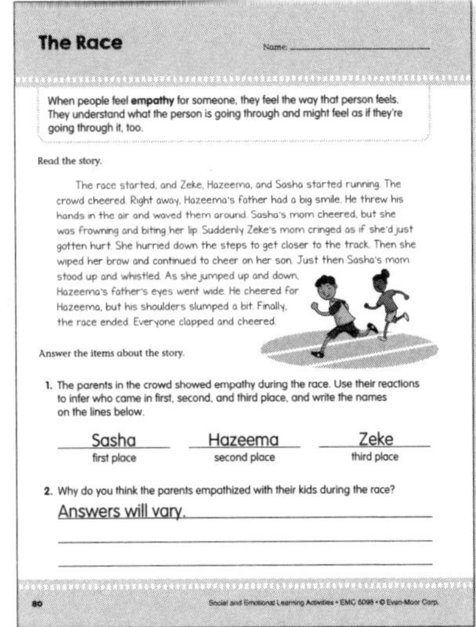

The Race Name: ______

When people feel **empathy** for someone, they feel the way that person feels. They understand what the person is going through and might feel as if they're going through it, too.

Read the story.

The race started, and Zeke, Hazeema, and Sasha started running. The crowd cheered. Right away, Hazeema's father had a big smile. He threw his hands in the air and waved them around. Sasha's mom cheered, but she was frowning and biting her lip. Suddenly Zeke's mom cringed as if she'd just gotten hurt. She hurried down the steps to get closer to the track. Then she wiped her brow and continued to cheer on her son. Just then Sasha's mom stood up and whistled. As she jumped up and down, Hazeema's father's eyes went wide. He cheered for Hazeema, but his shoulders slumped a bit. Finally, the race ended. Everyone clapped and cheered.

Answer the items about the story.

1. The parents in the crowd showed empathy during the race. Use their reactions to infer who came in first, second, and third place, and write the names on the lines below.

Sasha (first place) Hazeema (second place) Zeke (third place)

2. Why do you think the parents empathized with their kids during the race?
Answers will vary.

80 Social and Emotional Learning Activities • EMC 6098 • © Evan-Moor Corp.

Page 81

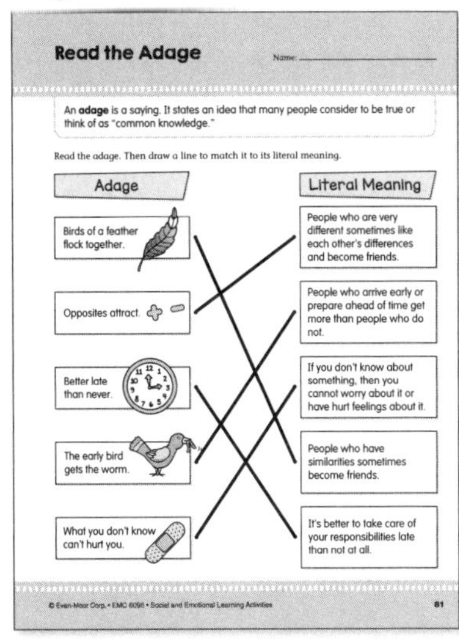

Read the Adage Name: ______

An **adage** is a saying. It states an idea that many people consider to be true or think of as "common knowledge."

Read the adage. Then draw a line to match it to its literal meaning.

Adage	Literal Meaning
Birds of a feather flock together.	People who have similarities sometimes become friends.
Opposites attract.	People who are very different sometimes like each other's differences and become friends.
Better late than never.	It's better to take care of your responsibilities late than not at all.
The early bird gets the worm.	People who arrive early or prepare ahead of time get more than people who do not.
What you don't know can't hurt you.	If you don't know about something, then you cannot worry about it or have hurt feelings about it.

© Evan-Moor Corp. • EMC 6098 • Social and Emotional Learning Activities 81

Page 84

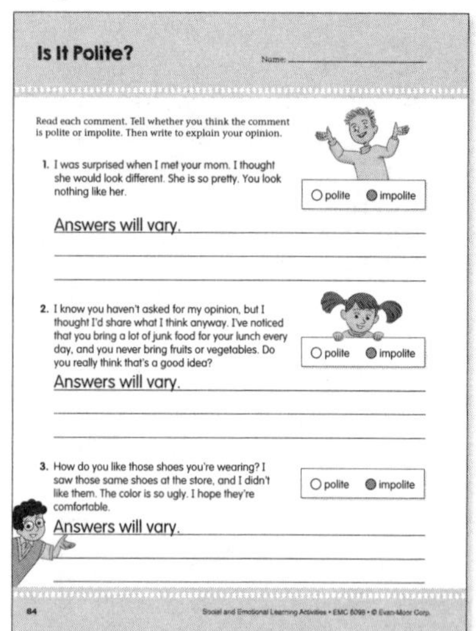

Is It Polite? Name: ______

Read each comment. Tell whether you think the comment is polite or impolite. Then write to explain your opinion.

1. I was surprised when I met your mom. I thought she would look different. She is so pretty. You look nothing like her. ○ polite ● impolite
   Answers will vary.
2. I know you haven't asked for my opinion, but I thought I'd share what I think anyway. I've noticed that you bring a lot of junk food for your lunch every day, and you never bring fruits or vegetables. Do you really think that's a good idea? ○ polite ● impolite
   Answers will vary.
3. How do you like those shoes you're wearing? I saw those same shoes at the store, and I didn't like them. The color is so ugly. I hope they're comfortable. ○ polite ● impolite
   Answers will vary.

84 Social and Emotional Learning Activities • EMC 6098 • © Evan-Moor Corp.

Page 86

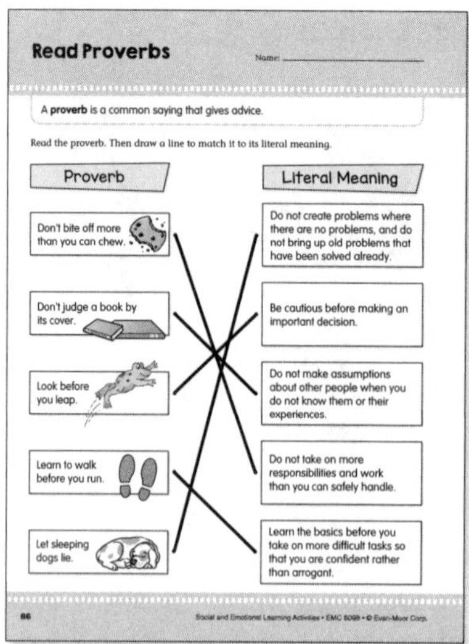

Read Proverbs Name: ______

A **proverb** is a common saying that gives advice.

Read the proverb. Then draw a line to match it to its literal meaning.

Proverb	Literal Meaning
Don't bite off more than you can chew.	Do not create problems where there are no problems, and do not bring up old problems that have been solved already.
Don't judge a book by its cover.	Be cautious before making an important decision.
Look before you leap.	Do not make assumptions about other people when you do not know them or their experiences.
Learn to walk before you run.	Do not take on more responsibilities and work than you can safely handle.
Let sleeping dogs lie.	Learn the basics before you take on more difficult tasks so that you are confident rather than arrogant.

86 Social and Emotional Learning Activities • EMC 6098 • © Evan-Moor Corp.

Page 89

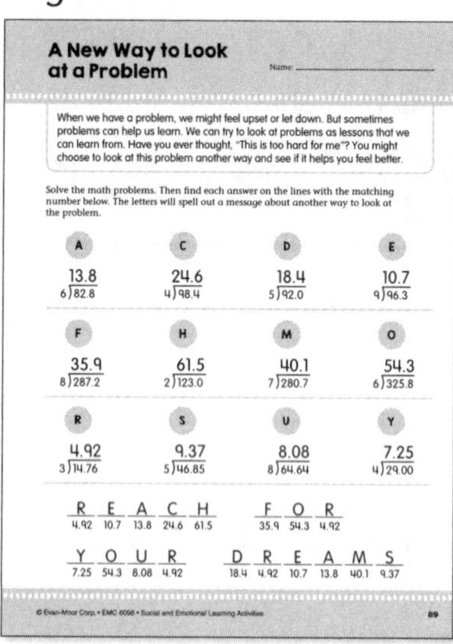

A New Way to Look at a Problem Name: ______

When we have a problem, we might feel upset or let down. But sometimes problems can help us learn. We can try to look at problems as lessons that we can learn from. Have you ever thought, "This is too hard for me"? You might choose to look at this problem another way and see if it helps you feel better.

Solve the math problems. Then find each answer on the lines with the matching number below. The letters will spell out a message about another way to look at the problem.

A	C	D	E
13.8 = 82.8 ÷ 6	24.6 = 98.4 ÷ 4	18.4 = 92.0 ÷ 5	10.7 = 96.3 ÷ 9
F	**H**	**M**	**O**
35.9 = 287.2 ÷ 8	61.5 = 123.0 ÷ 2	40.1 = 280.7 ÷ 7	54.3 = 325.8 ÷ 6
R	**S**	**U**	**Y**
4.92 = 14.76 ÷ 3	9.37 = 46.85 ÷ 5	8.08 = 64.64 ÷ 8	7.25 = 29.00 ÷ 4

R (4.92) E (10.7) A (13.8) C (24.6) H (61.5)   F (35.9) O (54.3) R (4.92)

Y (7.25) O (54.3) U (8.08) R (4.92)   D (18.4) R (4.92) E (10.7) A (13.8) M (40.1) S (9.37)

© Evan-Moor Corp. • EMC 6098 • Social and Emotional Learning Activities 89

Page 91

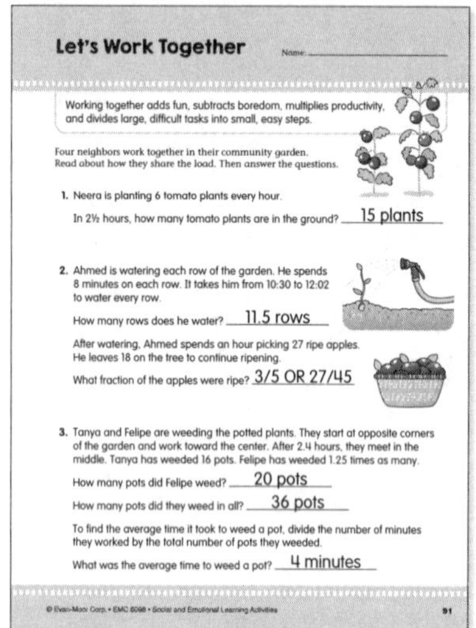

Let's Work Together Name: ______

Working together adds fun, subtracts boredom, multiplies productivity, and divides large, difficult tasks into small, easy steps.

Four neighbors work together in their community garden. Read about how they share the load. Then answer the questions.

1. Neera is planting 6 tomato plants every hour.
   In 2½ hours, how many tomato plants are in the ground? 15 plants
2. Ahmed is watering each row of the garden. He spends 8 minutes on each row. It takes him from 10:30 to 12:02 to water every row.
   How many rows does he water? 11.5 rows
   After watering, Ahmed spends an hour picking 27 ripe apples. He leaves 18 on the tree to continue ripening.
   What fraction of the apples were ripe? 3/5 OR 27/45
3. Tanya and Felipe are weeding the potted plants. They start at opposite corners of the garden and work toward the center. After 2.4 hours, they meet in the middle. Tanya has weeded 16 pots. Felipe has weeded 1.25 times as many.
   How many pots did Felipe weed? 20 pots
   How many pots did they weed in all? 36 pots
   To find the average time it took to weed a pot, divide the number of minutes they worked by the total number of pots they weeded.
   What was the average time to weed a pot? 4 minutes

© Evan-Moor Corp. • EMC 6098 • Social and Emotional Learning Activities 91

Page 106

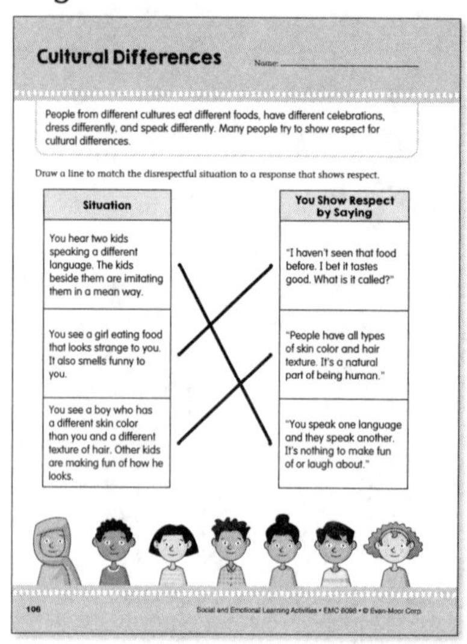

Cultural Differences Name: ______

People from different cultures eat different foods, have different celebrations, dress differently, and speak differently. Many people try to show respect for cultural differences.

Draw a line to match the disrespectful situation to a response that shows respect.

Situation	You Show Respect by Saying
You hear two kids speaking a different language. The kids beside them are imitating them in a mean way.	"I haven't seen that food before. I bet it tastes good. What is it called?"
You see a girl eating food that looks strange to you. It also smells funny to you.	"People have all types of skin color and hair texture. It's a natural part of being human."
You see a boy who has a different skin color than you and a different texture of hair. Other kids are making fun of how he looks.	"You speak one language and they speak another. It's nothing to make fun of or laugh about."

106 Social and Emotional Learning Activities • EMC 6098 • © Evan-Moor Corp.